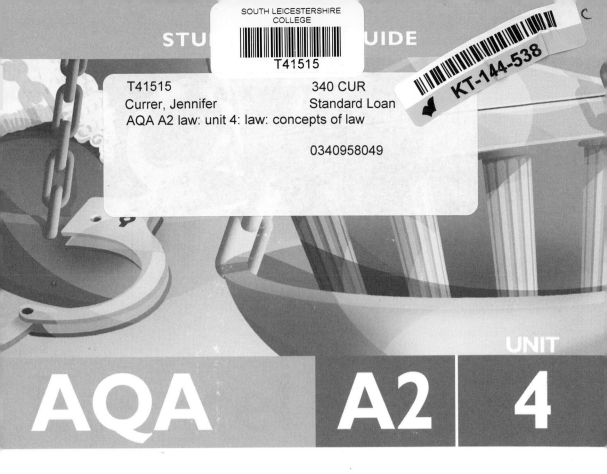

STU UIDE

AQA

A2 | UNIT 4

Law

Concepts of Law

Jennifer Currer and Peter Darwent

Philip Allan Updates, an imprint of Hodder Education, an Hachette UK company, Market Place, Deddington, Oxfordshire OX15 0SE

Orders

Bookpoint Ltd, 130 Milton Park, Abingdon, Oxfordshire OX14 4SB
tel: 01235 827720
fax: 01235 400454
e-mail: uk.orders@bookpoint.co.uk

Lines are open 9.00 a.m.–5.00 p.m., Monday to Saturday, with a 24-hour message answering service. You can also order through the Philip Allan Updates website: www.philipallan.co.uk

© Philip Allan Updates 2009

ISBN 978-0-340-95804-9

First printed 2009
Impression number 5 4 3 2
Year   2014 2013 2012 2011 2010

This guide has been written specifically to support students preparing for the AQA A2 Law Unit 4 examination. The content has been neither approved nor endorsed by AQA and remains the sole responsibility of the authors.

Typeset by Phoenix Photosetting, Chatham, Kent
Printed by MPG Books, Bodmin

Hachette UK's policy is to use papers that are natural, renewable and recyclable products and made from wood grown in sustainable forests. The logging and manufacturing processes are expected to conform to the environmental regulations of the country of origin.

Contents

Introduction

■ ■ ■

Content Guidance

■ ■ ■

Questions and Answers

Introduction

About this guide

The AQA specification for the AS and A2 Law examinations is divided into four mod-ules. The guide for Unit 4 Concepts of Law is different from the guides for Units 1, 2, 3 and Unit 4 Tort Law and Property Offences. While it does contain specific material on the concepts of law and morality, law and justice, fault, judicial creativity and balancing conflicting interests, it is essential that, in order to demonstrate knowledge and under-standing of these particular topics, you utilise appropriate knowledge of legal processes, institutions and substantive law gained in the study of the other modules.

Within this unit, you are also required to criticise and evaluate existing legal rules and to consider them in wider contexts — social, ethical and political.

There are three sections to this guide:

- **Introduction** — this provides advice on how the guide should be used, an explana-tion of the skills required to complete the unit successfully and guidance on revision and examination techniques.
- **Content Guidance** — this sets out the specification content for Unit 4 Concepts of Law. It also contains references to different materials drawn from previously stud-ied units to enable you to demonstrate a fuller understanding of each Unit 4 topic.
- **Questions and Answers** — this section provides sample A-grade answers to typi-cal examination questions on each topic area. Examiner comments show how marks are awarded.

How to use this guide

The Content Guidance section covers all the elements of the Unit 4 Concepts of Law specification. Given the nature of this unit, it must be stressed that this section is not intended to be a comprehensive and detailed set of notes — the material needs to be supplemented by further reading from textbooks, and illustrative material needs to be augmented by considering relevant examples from materials previously studied. You are also strongly encouraged to read quality newspapers on a regular basis, and to use relevant legal websites and law journals, especially *A-level Law Review*, *New Law Jour-nal* and other student magazines that give updates on legal developments.

Revision

Make sure you have a complete and accurate set of notes. Then, summarise all the material, organising it under the headings and subheadings of the Unit 4 specification.

During the revision period, you should go over your notes and reduce them to manageable proportions. The process of summarising makes it easier to recall the material and should reduce the chances of forgetting parts of it in the examination. More exam marks are lost through failure to provide fuller explanations than through any other factor.

Examination technique

Familiarise yourself with the style of questions for this unit. Learn from these questions and the AQA mark scheme what the Potential Content is for each question, and how marks are allocated across the different mark bands. The last section of this guide — Questions and Answers — is designed to provide guidance about the techniques required for this unit.

Time planning

Contrary to popular belief, few students have a problem with lack of time in the examination. By doing homework essays and timed or practice examination essays you will learn whether you are a slow or quick writer and how to plan and write full answers in no more than 55–60 minutes. Remember this examination lasts for 2 hours — 30 minutes longer than for Units 1, 2 and 3. While only 30 marks are allocated to the concepts of law question, the advice from AQA is clear. In the new specification, it states that the response to the concepts question is 'an hour-long essay', and your answers will be marked accordingly.

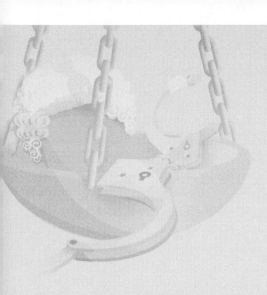

Content
Guidance

The specification for Unit 4 outlined in this section covers the following topics:

Law and morality
- Characteristics of legal rules
- Characteristics of moral rules
- Distinctions between legal and moral rules
- The relationship between legal and moral rules
- Coincidence of legal and moral rules
- Divergence of legal and moral rules
- Natural law theorists
- Positivists
- The Hart–Fuller debate
- The Hart–Devlin debate

Law and justice
- The meaning of 'justice'
- Theories of justice
- The extent to which substantive legal rules, legal institutions and processes achieve justice

Judicial creativity
- Characteristics of the doctrine of precedent which limit judicial creativity
- Characteristics of the doctrine of precedent which aid judicial creativity
- The extent to which judges are able to display creativity in statutory interpretation
- The balance between the roles of Parliament and the judiciary
- Policy
- Should judges create law?
- Judicial preference

Fault
- The meaning of 'fault'
- Fault in criminal law
- Fault in the law of tort
- Should liability in criminal law depend on proof of fault?
- Should liability in civil law depend on proof of fault?

Balancing conflicting interests
- Theorists
- Balancing of conflicting interests by Parliament
- Balancing of conflicting interests by the courts
- Balancing conflicting interests in criminal law
- Balancing conflicting interests in the law of tort

Law and morality

Characteristics of legal rules

Sir John Salmond, writing in the early twentieth century, described law as 'the body of principles recognised and applied by the state in the administration of justice'. John Austin, in his book *The Province of Jurisprudence*, defined it as a command issued from a sovereign power to an inferior and enforced by coercion. In Britain this sovereign power is Parliament, although legal rules are also made by judges.

Compliance with legal rules is compulsory. They are imposed on all members of society and must be obeyed. In Britain, everyone is bound by the **Offences Against the Person Act 1861**, s.20, which stipulates that people cannot intentionally or recklessly cause serious harm to another. The same principle applies to judicial decisions, for example *R* v *R* (1991), which established that a man could be found guilty of raping his wife.

Breach of legal rules will result in state sanctions and procedures. For example, breach of the criminal law may result in being arrested, charged and prosecuted through the criminal courts. If a person is found guilty, a criminal sanction, such as a fine, may be imposed. With reference to the **Offences Against the Person Act 1861**, for example, breach of s.20 may result in a maximum sentence of 5 years' imprisonment.

Legal rules are created and take effect at a precise time. A precedent is found in the judgement of a case and applies to future cases in lower courts. A piece of legislation/delegated legislation will take effect on a specified commencement date. For example, the **Smoke-free (Premises and Enforcement) Regulations**, made on 13 December 2006, came into force on 1 July 2007.

> **Tip**
> Examples of laws from virtually any part of the specification can be cited here.

Characteristics of moral rules

Phil Harris, in *An Introduction to Law*, defines a society's 'code of morality' as a set of beliefs, values, principles and standards of behaviour.

Compliance with moral rules is not required by the state. People may be influenced by family, friends or religion, or may choose for themselves what they consider to be moral or immoral.

Society is pluralistic. What one person considers immoral, another may not. For example, some people may believe that sex before marriage is immoral, while others consider it to be acceptable.

Moral rules develop gradually. They often stem from religious rules made thousands of years ago. Over time, conduct once considered immoral increasingly becomes acceptable. For example, the attitude towards homosexuality continues to change.

Moral rules are enforced informally, usually through social or domestic pressure. A person who repeatedly tells lies or breaks promises, for example, may be shunned or ostracised by friends, family or work colleagues.

Distinctions between legal and moral rules

Many of the distinctions between legal and moral rules emerge through a discussion of their characteristics. It is useful, however, to consider the following distinctions:
- Disagreement regarding the content of a legal rule can be resolved through reference to a precedent or Act of Parliament. This cannot be done with moral rules. Moral rules are not scientific truths and can be argued.
- Legal rules can be changed instantly, whereas moral rules evolve gradually. The legal rules regarding homosexual acts in private between consenting adults were instantly changed when the **Sexual Offences Act 1967** was passed. Society's moral acceptance of homosexuality, however, underwent and continues to undergo gradual change.
- Legal rules are enforced by state sanctions and procedures. Moral rules are enforced through social and domestic pressure, and are sometimes supported not by threats of punishment but by a reminder of the rules' existence, and by an implied appeal to respect them.
- Legal rules can impose strict liability. This can be seen in both criminal and civil law. For example, selling lottery tickets to persons under the age of 16 (*Harrow LBC v Shah,* 1999) is a strict liability offence. In civil law, the tort of nuisance is concerned with preventing interference with the enjoyment of proprietary interests. Moral offences, however, can only be committed voluntarily, with full *mens rea*.
- Due to the pluralistic nature of society, the moral codes of the various groups making up British society vary. However, all members of society are obliged to comply with legal rules.

The relationship between legal and moral rules

Any legal system presupposes a certain amount of morality, because if law is not essentially moral there is no easy explanation of the obligation to obey. The relationship between law and morality can perhaps best be described as two intersecting circles. The area inside the intersection represents the coincidence of law and morality, and the areas outside represent areas of divergence.

> **Tip**
>
> You are required to explore both the coincidence and the divergence of legal and moral rules. Better answers will provide discussion of a wide range of issues and will show understanding of the complex relationship between law and morality. It is important to consider the variety of ways in which the two can relate to each other. For example, the report on the January 2003 examination commented on the fact that not one candidate considered the possibility of legal rules influencing a change in moral rules.

Coincidence of legal and moral rules

Long-established legal rules influenced by moral rules

There are many long-established rules which have a moral connection. These include the laws of murder and theft, which can be traced back to the Ten Commandments.

Public morality may influence judicial change

Criminal law
- The decision in *R* v *R* (1991) was influenced by the moral rule that a husband should not be able to force his wife to have sexual intercourse.
- The decision in *R* v *Brown* (1993) was influenced by the moral rule that holds sadomasochistic activities as being unacceptable, even if consented to.

Contract law
In *Central London Property* v *High Trees House* (1947), Lord Denning created the equitable remedy of promissory estoppel, the basis of which is that people ought not to break their promises.

The law of tort
The decision in *Chadwick* v *British Railways Board* (1967) was influenced by the moral rule that people ought to help others who may be in trouble.

Public morality may influence legislative reform

Many legislative reforms of the 1960s could be said to reflect the 'permissive' moral ideals of that decade. Abortion was legalised by the **Abortion Act 1967**, and the **Sexual Offences Act 1967** legalised homosexual acts in private between consenting adults. The law responded to the continued shift in public morality by reducing the homosexual age of consent, first to 18 in 1994, and then to 16 in 2000. Adoption legislation enacted in 2002 gives gay couples the right to adopt a child, and the **Civil**

Partnership Act 2004 allows civil registrations that give gay and lesbian couples the same legal entitlements as marriage in areas such as employment, pensions and social security. However, the 2004 Act does not allow religious ceremonies.

The law is often slow to respond, as is evident in the reluctance to decriminalise assisted suicide. The conclusions of the British Social Attitudes Survey 2007 found that 80% of the population is in favour of assisted suicide if it is helped by a doctor. In July 2009 there was a landmark legal victory in the House of Lords for Debbie Purdy, a woman with multiple sclerosis who claimed that it was a breach of her human rights not knowing if her husband would be prosecuted if he accompanies her to the Swiss 'suicide clinic' Dignitas. The Law Lords ruled that the director of public prosecutions must set out a policy on this difficult subject.

Public morality may be influenced by law reform

It can be argued that some legislation is introduced partly with the aim of educating the public to consider certain matters unacceptable, i.e. morally wrong. Discrimination legislation, for example, aims to educate people to regard treating others differently on the grounds of sex, race or disability as wrong.

Law reform may be the product of a campaign to change public morality

In 1949, the Howard League for Penal Reform persuaded the government to appoint a Royal Commission on Capital Punishment. The Howard League then persuaded most members of the Commission to be in favour of the abolition of the death penalty. The government refused to implement the proposals because public opinion considered the death penalty to be morally correct. Subsequently, a pressure group called the National Campaign for the Abolition of Capital Punishment was set up. During the years 1955–57, public opinion was changed by the campaign and the government introduced the necessary legislation to abolish the death penalty.

The pluralistic nature of society means coincidence is partial

In England, there is a large population of mixed cultures, races, political ideals and religious followings. This leads to significant divergence of views on a number of moral issues. For example, some people regard abortion as immoral, while others feel it is acceptable for medical reasons only. There is disagreement among those in favour of abortion about the stage of pregnancy at which the procedure is acceptable. Such a divergence of views was expressed at the second reading of the Human Fertilisation and Embryology Bill in May 2008, in which MPs voted against reducing the current 24-week abortion limit to 20 weeks by 332 votes to 190. MPs voting to retain the 24-week limit were concerned to preserve access to safe, legal abortion. Some MPs in favour of reducing the limit were persuaded by recent research indicating that some fetuses are viable at 23 or 22 weeks' gestation, while other MPs, largely influenced by religious beliefs, favoured a reduction to 12 weeks.

It can be argued that there is no public moral consensus on many moral issues. Further examples to consider are *Gillick* v *West Norfolk and Wisbech Area Health Authority* (1986), *Re A (Children)* (2000) and the Diane Pretty and Debbie Purdy cases, which both raised the issue of assisted suicide.

Reasons for the overlap between legal and moral rules

Legal and moral rules are concerned with imposing certain standards of conduct, without which society would break down. In many of these fundamental standards, law and morality reinforce and supplement each other as part of the fabric of social life. For example, sanctions and remedies imposed by the law reinforce moral disapproval of breaches of legal rules that forbid immoral acts.

Therefore, legal rules do not exist in a vacuum, but, as Harris writes, 'are found side by side with moral codes of greater or less complexity. The relationship of law to moral rules and standards is therefore one of great and abiding importance in every human society, and certainly not least in our own'.

The close link between legal rules and moral rules is also demonstrated by the similarity of normative language that each employs. Both are concerned to lay down rules or 'norms' of conduct for human beings, and this is expressed both in moral and legal language in terms of obligations, duties, or of what is right or wrong.

Divergence of legal and moral rules

Some legal rules appear to have no moral connection

There appears to be little moral justification for the fact that tobacco and alcohol consumption are legal while smoking cannabis is illegal. Likewise, what is the moral justification for closing pubs at 11p.m.? And is it morally wrong to park on yellow lines or drive on a motorway at 72 miles per hour? There are some arguments, however, against the assertion that such laws have no connection with morals. It may be considered immoral, for example, to park in disabled parking spaces if you are not actually disabled or to partially block roads, making access difficult for emergency services vehicles.

Some moral rules have little or no legal backing

While there is a moral duty to help those who may be in danger, the general position of the law is that there is no liability for an omission to act. For example, the passer-by who fails to rescue someone who is drowning will not be held responsible. However, there are some exceptions in criminal law to this rule, such as when a person creates the danger, as in the case of *R* v *Miller* (1983), or where there is an assumption of responsibility, a special relationship or a contractual duty to act.

The remedy of promissory estoppel, considered earlier, is an exception to the general position of the law that there is no legal requirement to keep a promise. There is, however, a moral duty to do so.

Reasons for the divergence between legal and moral rules

As can be seen from the previous examples, the law often shrinks from pursuing what may be recognised as the path of morality. The reasons for this vary. It may be because the moral attitude is not sufficiently widespread, and the law would not reflect popular morality. It may also be because there are fields of human activity where the law deliberately prefers to abstain from supporting the moral rule because it is felt that the machinery of enforcement is too cumbersome to deal with the moral wrong — more social harm may be created than prevented by legal intervention. This was the reason why the Wolfenden Committee recommended that private homosexual behaviour should be decriminalised.

It was also the reason the legislature delayed making forced marriages illegal. The government was concerned about offending cultural sensitivities. However, as the then minister for racial equality stated: 'The government must respond sensitively to the issues of cultural diversity, but multicultural sensitivity is no excuse for moral blindness.' The **Forced Marriage (Civil Protection) Act 2007** came into effect in November 2008, making it an offence to force someone into marriage.

Natural law theorists

Natural law theorists argue that, in order to be valid, the law must coincide with natural law. Throughout history, many different views have been expressed as to what natural law is.

In the fourth century BC, the Greek philosopher Aristotle based his theory of natural law on the law of nature. He believed that the principles which governed the universe, and which explained how it was structured and how it functioned, could be discovered through observation and the power of human reason.

By the Middle Ages, natural law theorists believed that the natural law was the divine law or the law of God. St Thomas Aquinas, writing in the thirteenth century, expressed the view that the universe was created by God, and that when God created man he enabled him to know the truth. According to Aquinas, man is able to discover the truth of divine law through revelation, for example in the Holy Scriptures, through reflection, and through practical reasoning. Aquinas believed that if human law was at variance with the divine law, it was not legal but rather a corruption of the law.

In more recent times, the influence of the church has arguably declined. Professor Lon Fuller, in his book *Morality of Law* (1964), refers to what he terms the 'inner morality of law'. For Fuller, any legal system is only valid if it conforms to certain procedural requirements, including that law must be understandable and that it must not be retrospective. Many aspects of the English legal system do not comply with Fuller's requirements. For example, some legislation is not understandable even by the judiciary, and judicial law-making is retrospective. While the decision in *R* v *R* (1991) was welcomed because it reflected public morality, it was retrospective in effect. In *R* v *Crooks* (2004), the Court of Appeal upheld the conviction (in 2002) of the defendant, who had had sexual intercourse with his wife without her consent in 1970, 21 years before such behaviour was made a criminal offence.

While it can be seen that views expressed as to what natural law is have varied, there is nevertheless a common thread. As Lord Lloyd of Hampstead points out in *Introduction to Jurisprudence*: 'What has remained constant is an assertion that there are principles of natural law...the essence of natural law may be said to lie in the constant assertion that there are objective moral principles which depend upon the nature of the universe and which can be discovered by reason.'

Positivists

Jeremy Bentham

Jeremy Bentham (1748–1832) rejected natural law theories as being 'nonsense upon stilts'. His key criticisms were that natural law was based upon unprovable principles, and that natural law theorists confused legal issues with moral issues. For Bentham, the validity of a law did not depend on whether it was good or bad. What the law is and what the law ought to be should be treated as different issues. Bentham was primarily concerned with the promotion of the utility principle, i.e. the greatest happiness for the greatest number. However, a law not promoting this principle would not automatically be adjudged to be invalid.

John Austin

John Austin (1790–1859) is credited with formulating the first coherent theory of positivism. He rejected the principle of natural law, whereby validity of law is dependent upon it not being in conflict with a 'higher law', be it natural or divine. For Austin, a law may be valid irrespective of its moral content. He defined law in terms of a command from a sovereign, whom the bulk of society is in the habit of obeying, enforced by a sanction. The origins of the command theory can be traced to Bentham and to Hobbes (1588–1679).

H. L. A. Hart

Professor Hart, in his book *The Concept of Law* (1963), also subscribes to the positivist view, while being critical of some aspects of Austin's command theory.

The Hart–Fuller debate

The Hart–Fuller debate took place during the years 1958–67. In essence, it was a response of both natural law theory and positivism to the views expressed by the

German philosopher Gustav Radbruch, on the validity of laws passed under the Nazi regime. Radbruch had been a positivist prior to the Nazi era, but the atrocities perpetrated, apparently with legal approval, during that period led him to believe that no law could be valid if it contravened basic moral principles.

Following the Second World War, many informers were tried as war criminals. In their defence they typically argued that what they were doing was legal, as the law at that time made it illegal to make statements which were detrimental to the government. The approach of the German courts was to declare these Nazi laws invalid as they were 'contrary to the sound conscience and sense of justice of all decent human beings'. This approach was clearly in agreement with the natural law theorists and Fuller supported it.

Hart disagreed with Fuller. According to Hart, the law was valid despite being so fundamentally contrary to moral principles. Hart did not disagree that the law was immoral, only that it was invalid.

The Hart–Devlin debate

The issue of how far law and morals should coincide was widely discussed in the late 1950s, when there was public concern about an apparent decline in sexual morality. This became known as the Hart–Devlin debate, not to be confused with the Hart–Fuller debate, which was concerned with the validity of legal rules that conflict with moral rules. The Hart–Devlin debate was concerned with the extent to which the law should enforce moral rules.

Statements reflecting the pluralistic nature of society can be found in the debates surrounding the legal reforms of the 1960s. The **Sexual Offences Act 1967**, which legalised homosexuality, was introduced following recommendations made by the Wolfenden Committee in its 1957 report. Two years after the publication of the Wolfenden Report, Lord Devlin, in his book, *The Enforcement of Morals*, set out his criticisms of the Wolfenden recommendations. In 1962, Professor Hart set out his arguments against Devlin's views in his book, *Law, Liberty and Morality*.

Professor Hart drew on the work of John Stuart Mill who, in his essay 'On liberty' (1859), stated: 'The only part of the conduct of anyone, for which he is amenable to society, is that which concerns others. In the part which merely concerns himself, his independence, is of right, absolute. Over himself, over his own body and mind, the individual is sovereign.' John Stuart Mill and Professor Hart put forward the view that the minority should not be made to conform to the will of the majority when in private, as this would amount to tyranny and be immoral. They thus recognised the pluralistic nature of society.

Professor Hart argued that using law to enforce moral values was unnecessary, undesirable and morally unacceptable: unnecessary because society was capable of containing many moral standpoints without disintegrating; undesirable because it would freeze morality at a particular point; and morally unacceptable because it infringes the freedom of the individual. He also pointed out that objections to unusual behaviour are often prompted by ignorance, prejudice and misunderstanding.

Sir James Stephen, a leading criminal judge in the late nineteenth century, disagreed with Mill. In his work *Liberty, Equality, Fraternity* (1874) he stated:

> I think that the attempt to distinguish between self-regarding acts and acts which regard others is like an attempt to distinguish between acts which happen in time and acts which happen in space. Every act happens at some time and in some space, and, in like manner, every act that we do either does or may affect both ourselves and others. I therefore think that the distinction is altogether fallacious and unfounded.

He went on to say: 'There are acts of wickedness so gross and outrageous that they must be punished at any cost to the offender.' Stephen's view was that the prevention of immoral behaviour was an end in itself.

Lord Devlin's views are more in line with those of Sir James Stephen. While Devlin believed that individual privacy should be respected, he stated: 'History shows that the loosening of moral bonds is often the first stage of disintegration...suppression of vice is as much the law's business as the suppression of subversive activities.' He believed that society shared a common morality and that the law should intervene to punish acts which offend that shared morality, whether done in public or private. Failure to intervene would result in the disintegration of society. He argued that individual liberty could only flourish in a stable society; disintegration of society through lack of a shared morality would, therefore, threaten individual freedom.

Tip

This debate must be discussed in relation to the coincidence of legal and moral rules. Better candidates will demonstrate detailed knowledge of the views of both Professor Hart and Lord Devlin, and will be able to explain how the debate has influenced the law in more recent years.

The influence of Mill–Hart

Sir John Wolfenden followed the views of Mill and Hart, recognising the pluralistic nature of society and the importance of individual liberty. The resulting legislation, the **Sexual Offences Act 1967**, legalising homosexuality, was thus influenced by the views of Mill and Hart. Their views were also reflected in other reforming legislation of that period such as the **Obscene Publications Act 1968** and the **Divorce Law Reform Act 1969**.

The majority of the House of Lords in *Gillick v Norfolk and Wisbech Area Health Authority* (1986) also adopted the Mill–Hart approach. They held that it was legal for doctors to offer contraceptive advice and treatment to girls under the age of 16 without parental consent, provided they were satisfied that the girls had sufficient understanding of the issues involved. Lord Scarman said that 'parental rights are derived from parental duty' and that the 'dwindling right' of a parent as the child grows older 'yields to the child's right to make his own decision when he reaches a sufficient understanding and intelligence to be capable of making up his own mind on the matter requiring decision'.

More recently, the European Court of Human Rights was influenced by the Mill–Hart approach in *ADT* v *UK* (2000). The European Court of Human Rights ruled that the conviction of a man who engaged in non-violent consensual homosexual acts in private with up to four other men was a violation of Article 8 — the right to respect for private life.

The influence of Stephen–Devlin

The dissenting judgements of Lords Brandon and Templeman in *Gillick* v *Norfolk and Wisbech Area Health Authority* (1986) reflected concerns over the wider social implications. Lord Brandon's dissent was based largely on the question of public policy and his concern for the criminal aspect in terms of underage sex. Lord Templeman ignored case law and produced an opinion, the most memorable line of which is: 'There are many things which a girl under 16 needs to practise but sex is not one of them.' These views were an echo of Lord Devlin's concern about social disintegration.

The influence of Stephen and Devlin can be seen in a number of other judicial decisions. In *Shaw* v *DPP* (1962), the Ladies' Directory case, the House of Lords ruled that a publication advertising the services of prostitutes was a conspiracy to corrupt public morals. Viscount Simmonds argued: 'In the sphere of criminal law I entertain no doubt that there remains in the courts a residual power to enforce the supreme and fundamental purpose of the law, to conserve not only the safety and order, but also the moral welfare of the state.'

More recent decisions show that there is still judicial support for the Devlin viewpoint that some acts are intrinsically immoral, regardless of whether they harm others. In *R* v *Gibson* (1990) an artist exhibited earrings made from freeze-dried fetuses of 3–4 months' gestation. A conviction for the common law offence of outraging public decency was upheld.

Perhaps the most significant recent decisions are those of the House of Lords in *R* v *Brown* (1993) and the European Court of Human Rights (ECtHR) in *Laskey, Brown and Jaggard* v *United Kingdom* (1997). In the House of Lords case, the question was whether the defence of consent could be used in respect of sadomasochistic acts. The people involved were consenting adults and none of the activities were conducted in public or had resulted in the need for medical treatment. The activities concerned included whipping, caning, branding and nailing their genitals to pieces of wood. The House of Lords held that the defence of consent could not be applied to such practices and that such behaviour was not to be encouraged by relaxation of the law. When the defendants took their case to the ECtHR they lost on the basis that there was no breach of Article 8, as infringement of the right to respect for private life was justified by the need to protect health or morals. This approach was followed in *R* v *Emmett* (1999). A woman consented to her partner covering her head with a plastic bag, tying it tightly at the neck, and to him pouring lighter fuel on her breasts and setting them alight. The court held her consent did not provide a defence to her partner.

Conclusion

One of the difficulties for the law is that not only is society pluralistic, but also that views are sometimes passionately held, allowing little scope for compromise. In general terms, it could be argued that a large section of society has come to adopt the view taken by Professor Hart, and inevitably this has been reflected in both legislative changes and in judicial decisions. On the other hand, significant groups remain opposed to what they perceive as a dangerous weakening of the moral basis of law.

> **Tip**
>
> Moral issues are always liable to figure prominently in the media, and you are encouraged to use whatever examples are currently in the news. Issues such as euthanasia, abortion, consent to violent sexual acts, animal rights, stem cell research and interventions in the field of human fertilisation remain contentious. New issues sometimes emerge, an example being forced marriage.

Law and justice

> **Tip**
>
> Most exam questions require you to explain in theory what justice is, and then to explain how far in practice justice is achieved. However, a common fault is to define justice well and to give examples of justice in operation, but not to link these two parts.

The meaning of 'justice'

'Justice' has many meanings. The definition given in the *Oxford English Dictionary* is 'just conduct; fairness', and this is the common understanding of the word. The definition of 'just' is 'acting or done in accordance with what is morally right or proper'. The definition of 'fair' is 'free from discrimination, dishonesty...in conformity with rules or standards'. Lord Lloyd emphasises the difficulty in defining justice precisely: 'Justice, whatever its precise meaning may be, is itself a moral value, that is one of the aims or purposes which man sets himself in order to attain the good life.' It would appear that conceptions of justice vary from age to age, person to person and according to existing economic relations.

Ch. Perelman recognised that justice has several meanings. In his book, *De La Justice* (1945), he set out six possible meanings of justice:

(1) 'To each according to his works' (rewards are based on contribution)

(2) 'To each according to his needs' (people receive what they need)

(3) 'To each according to his merits' (people get what they deserve)

(4) 'To each according to his rank' (people may enjoy privileges according to status)

(5) 'To each according to his legal entitlement' (people receive what the law says they should)

(6) 'To each equally' (all people receive the same)

While recognising that justice may have several meanings, Perelman believed that once the type of justice subscribed to by a society was identified, then all individuals had to be treated the same. He subscribed to the theory of formal justice.

Justice, according to the law, can be formal, substantive, distributive or corrective, or any combination of these types:

- Formal justice, often referred to as procedural justice, requires equality of treatment in accordance with the classification laid down by rules.
- Substantive justice is concerned with whether rules are just.
- Distributive justice is concerned with the fair allocation of benefits and burdens within society.
- Corrective justice requires the righting of wrongs through fair remedy or punishment.

Theories of justice

There are numerous theories of justice. It is important to be able to explain and evaluate these theories and their relationships with each other, and to understand their application to modern society.

Aristotle

The Greek philosopher Aristotle introduced the principles of distributive justice and corrective justice:

- The principle of distributive justice requires that the allocation of assets in society should be proportional to a person's claim on them. He argued that this did not necessarily mean equal shares.
- The principle of corrective justice requires that where distributive justice is disturbed by wrongdoing, there should be a means of restoring the original position. This might be done by imposing penalties or awarding compensation.

St Thomas Aquinas

Aquinas's **natural law theory** assumes that if higher law is followed, the result will be justice. An unjust law might be contrary to human good or against the higher law derived from God. A law which goes against this God-derived law will always be 'unjust' and should not be obeyed. Some Roman Catholics today would argue that this applies to laws legalising abortion. Members of many faith groups would find it difficult to obey laws that compelled them to break what they regard as fundamental principles. An interesting example that recognises this issue is the exemption given to Sikhs from the requirement to wear a crash helmet when riding a motorcycle.

Jeremy Bentham

The **theory of utilitarianism** was developed by Jeremy Bentham. The aim of utilitarianism is to maximise human happiness by increasing pleasure and diminishing pain. For the utilitarian, justice is concerned with promoting 'the greatest happiness of the greatest number'. The sum of human happiness is assessed by numerical means and each person's happiness is equal in value.

Utilitarianism has been influential in legal reform and appears to be based on democratic principles. In democratic societies, citizens must comply with laws made by a government elected by the majority. It is a secular theory. However, utilitarianism can be criticised for being difficult to apply in practice: it is questionable whether happiness can be directly or precisely measured. Another criticism is that utilitarianism is concerned with the consequences of an act and not the means by which it is achieved. Thus, torture may justify the end result of obtaining information. Individuals are not regarded as important and the complete misery of a few is justified if it increases the happiness of the many.

This is in conflict with other theories of justice, such as that of Rawls and Marx, who regard the rights of the individual as all-important.

Positivism

John Austin developed the ideas of Bentham. Like Bentham, Austin also rejected the principle of natural law. For Austin, a law may be valid irrespective of its moral content or whether it delivers justice. Professor Hart in *The Concept of Law* (1963) also subscribes to the positivist view. He argues that it is possible to administer unjust laws in a just manner and vice versa.

John Rawls

John Rawls in *A Theory of Justice* (1971) sets out justice as fairness:

> The main task clearly is to determine which principles of justice would be chosen in the original position…The idea of the original position is to set up a fair procedure so that any principles agreed to will be just…It seems reasonable to suppose that the parties in the original position are equal, that is, all have the same rights in the procedure for choosing principles; each can make proposals, submit reasons for their acceptance and so on….

In order to avoid the situation whereby people exploit social and natural circumstances to their own advantage, Rawls places these people in the original position behind a 'veil of ignorance', whereby 'the parties do not know certain kinds of particular facts. First of all, no one knows his place in society, his class position or social status; nor does he know his fortune in the distribution of natural assets and abilities, his intelligence and strength and the like'. Furthermore, people behind the veil of ignorance do not know what they will value as good or bad, or what economic or political situation, level of civilisation and culture are prevalent in their society. According to Rawls, two principles would be chosen from these circumstances: 'First: each person is to have an equal right to the most extensive basic liberty compatible with a similar liberty for others. Second: social and economic inequalities are to be arranged so that they are both (a) reasonably expected to be to everyone's advantage, and (b) attached to positions and offices open to all.'

Rawls rejects the notion of utility. He believes that justice is achieved through rules which create inequality only if that inequality is of benefit to all, not merely to the greatest number. Furthermore, the equal right to liberty cannot be denied in favour of greater social or economic advantages.

Rawls's theory of justice is reflected in both English law and in the European Convention on Human Rights. Rawls subscribes to liberalism, which is primarily concerned with freedom and the autonomy of individuals. The European Convention on Human Rights reflects this in that it ensures individuals are given the positive rights Rawls regards as important, including freedom of speech and assembly and freedom from arbitrary arrest and seizure. However, the derogation clauses depart from Rawls's theory, allowing for a denial of rights, for example 'in the interests of national security, public safety or the economic well-being of the country, for the prevention of disorder or crime, for the protection of health or morals, or for the protection of the rights and freedoms of others' (Article 8). Only the last point arguably reflects Rawls's theory, in that individual liberty can be limited if it will result in greater liberty overall.

Marxism

Karl Marx, like Rawls, subscribed to an ideal of justice rather than to an actual existing system. For Marx, the ideal society meant, 'From each according to his ability, to each according to his needs'. He argued that justice cannot be achieved until the ideal society is in place, for any other society is defective and justice therein impossible. However, Marx also propounded the view that: 'Once the new productive arrangements appear, there will be no need for principles of justice for production or distribution.' Justice for Marx would be the existence of his ideal society and there would apparently be no need for a law to conform to. Such sentiments were also expressed by eighteenth century theorist **David Hume**: 'If every man had a tender regard for another, or if nature supplied abundantly all our wants and desires...the jealousy of interest, which justice supposes, could no longer have place. Increase to a sufficient degree the benevolence of men, or the bounty of nature, and you render justice useless.' It is clear that Britain does not correspond to the ideal society as envisaged by either Hume or Marx.

Robert Nozick and the minimal state

Nozick rejected the distributive theories of justice of Rawls and Marx and instead developed the **entitlement theory** of justice, according to which goods arise already encumbered with ownership. He maintained that individuals have natural rights to the enjoyment of life, health, liberty and possessions, free from interference by others. Rather than being concerned with equality, the entitlement theory stipulates that the state should only intervene to protect natural rights: inequalities are a fact of life. It holds that the state should play a minimum role and is not justified in diminishing or increasing the natural rights which an individual possesses. Redistribution of individuals' rights is not justified for any social purpose. Legal systems such as that operating in the UK, which go further than merely enforcing natural rights, do not comply with Nozick's theory of justice.

Natural justice and the rule of law

It would be reasonable to claim that if a legal system is to be based on justice, it must incorporate the principles of natural justice and the rule of law.

Phil Harris, in *An Introduction to Law*, argues that the idea of natural justice 'has no mysterious or magical meaning: it simply refers to a duty to act fairly'. This is based on two requirements: that each party should have the opportunity to be heard and that no one should be judge in his own cause. This principle can be seen operating in *R v Bow Street Metropolitan Stipendiary Magistrates, ex parte Pinochet* (1999), in which the House of Lords decided that General Pinochet, the former dictator of Chile, should be extradited to Spain to face serious charges of human rights abuse. When it was revealed that Lord Hoffman, one of the Law Lords who heard the case, had links with Amnesty International, a human rights organisation involved in the proceedings, the House of Lords annulled the decision and reheard the case without Lord Hoffman.

The theory of the rule of law as outlined by Dicey in the nineteenth century is that 'no person is punishable except for a distinct breach of the law established in the courts' and also that no man is 'above the law, but that every man, whatever his rank, is subject to the ordinary law of the realm'.

The extent to which substantive legal rules, legal institutions and processes achieve justice

Tip

In questioning whether the English law complies with the requirements of formal and substantive justice, examples of rules, institutions and processes from many parts of the specification can be used. These examples can then be related to the meanings and theories of justice and examined in order to assess how successful they are in achieving justice. Andrew Mitchell in 'Exploring law and justice', *A-level Law Review*, Vol. 1, No. 2, provides a useful table of examples that can be used to illustrate aspects of the English legal system that reflect formal, substantive, distributive and corrective justice. He also recommends research into some miscarriages of justice.

Judicial review

One of the ways in which the rule of law is guaranteed is by having an independent judiciary able to review the decisions of politicians and public officials.

The process of judicial review does not examine the merits of a decision, but simply whether the body or individual in question was within their rights in making the decision. It is a means of formal justice. If a decision is *ultra vires* (goes beyond their powers), it can be quashed. Procedural *ultra vires* arises where proper procedures have not been followed, e.g. there has been a breach of natural justice, as in the Pinochet case. Substantive *ultra vires* arises where the content of the decision was outside the power of the body that made it. One of the problems with substantive *ultra vires* is that it is difficult for judges to control the actions of public bodies if the discretionary powers granted to such bodies are very wide. For example, in *R* v *Secretary of State for the Environment ex parte Norwich City Council* (1982), the wording of the **Housing Act 1980** allowed the Secretary of State to 'do all such things as appear to him necessary or expedient' to enable council house tenants to buy their council houses. The courts accepted that, in cases where sales were proceeding slowly, this gave him the right to remove the power from the local authority and exercise it himself.

It could be argued that the real test of whether a system is based on the principles of justice is how it copes with direct or perceived threats to national security. If principles that are regarded as sacred at other times are abandoned if there is perceived to be a threat to national security, it brings into question whether our system is based on justice. It has been suggested that the reliance by governments on the requirements of national security has inhibited judicial review of their decisions. In *R* v *Secretary of State for Home Affairs ex parte Hosenball* (1977), the Court of Appeal held that an American journalist could be deported, even though the rules of natural justice had not been followed, because the decision was made on the grounds of national security. Similarly, in *Council of Civil Service Unions* v *Minister for the Civil Service* (1985), the government decision to ban employees at the Government Communications Headquarters (GCHQ) from membership of trade unions was upheld on the basis that it claimed that it was necessary for reasons of national security.

However, the passing of the **Human Rights Act 1998** has enabled judges to review even primary legislation to determine whether it complies with the European Convention on Human Rights. In *A and Others* v *Secretary of State for the Home Department* (2004), the House of Lords took the view that the detention of foreign nationals without trial under s.21 of the **Anti-Terrorism, Crime and Security Act 2001** was not justified, even though the government argued that they were a threat to national security.

Judicial independence

Judicial independence is fundamental to the rule of natural justice that no one should be a judge in his or her own cause — *nemo judex in causa sua*. An aspect of judicial independence is that judges should be independent from the case. The example of the Pinochet case has already been mentioned.

Similarly, in *Morrison* v *AWG Group Ltd and another* (2006), the Court of Appeal held that a High Court judge should have stood down from hearing the case. He acknowledged that he had known a witness for some 30 years, and consequently that witness was replaced. The judge then heard the case. Lord Justice Mummery stated that in such situations judges should stand down to avoid any perception of bias, however unjustified such a perception might be.

Access to justice

The rules relating to equal access to justice in England seem to have become more substantially unjust in recent years. Government funding for legal cases was introduced by the **Legal Aid Act 1949**, with the aim of providing the means for everyone to have access to justice, rather than only those who could afford it. The system was means-tested and demand-led so that all those who applied would receive funding, provided they fell within the eligibility criteria. When the system was first introduced, approximately 80% of the population was eligible for some government funding; however, the expense to the taxpayer of this system persuaded successive governments to alter the means test so that fewer people qualified, and by the early 1990s only 40% of the population was eligible for legal aid.

The position has been improved to some extent by the **Access to Justice Act 1999**, but problems remain. The Act introduced a limit on the amount of funding available, so that when the money runs out, no further funding is available. The limits for eligibility remain low. There are also certain types of action excluded from the system, such as personal injury cases, although these can be pursued through conditional fee arrangements. However, not everyone will be able to find a lawyer willing to accept their case on a conditional fee. Lawyers are only willing to accept those cases they feel sure of winning.

The rules regarding government funding suggest that formal justice is denied. The law in general cannot be applied impartially if certain sections of society are denied access to it or are denied adequate legal representation. It can also be argued that such rules are substantially unjust because they have the effect of denying equal access.

The criminal justice system

The miscarriage of justice cases in the 1980s and 1990s, such as the Guildford Four, the Maguires and the Birmingham Six, raised questions about the way the criminal justice system was operating and suggested that in their eagerness to get convictions, the police had compromised some of the principles of formal justice. In particular, there were concerns about confessions and the treatment of the defendants while they were in custody and also about the reliability of forensic evidence.

When Judith Ward was cleared in 1992 after serving 18 years for the bombing of a coach on the M62 motorway, which killed 12 people, the Court of Appeal said that a grave miscarriage of justice had occurred:

> In failing to disclose evidence...the West Yorkshire police, the scientists who gave evidence at the trial, and some of those members of the staff of the DPP and counsel who advised them... failed to carry out their basic duty to seek to ensure a trial which is fair to both the prosecution...and the accused.

Arguably, however, the system did eventually deliver justice, because the appeal system led to the convictions in all these IRA cases, and in others, such as the Tottenham Three and the Bridgewater Four, being quashed and compensation being paid.

Justice for victims?

The Stephen Lawrence case demonstrates that there can also be concerns about whether the institutions of the state operate fairly in the interests of all those affected by crime. Victims, unlike defendants, do not get a second chance. The suspects were acquitted and a private prosecution was also unsuccessful. The acquittals in this case were influential in the 'double jeopardy' rule being relaxed. The **Criminal Justice Act 2003** allows for people acquitted of certain serious offences to be retried, provided both the DPP and the Court of Appeal are satisfied that there is 'new and compelling evidence' and that it is in the interests of justice to have a retrial.

The case of Damilola Taylor also focused on the sense of frustration felt by the families of victims when there are unsuccessful prosecutions. The response of the press to the acquittal of the defendants in the initial case, suggested in the words of the *Daily Mirror*, was that this was 'another murdered black boy betrayed by British justice'. But David Pannick, in an article in *The Times* (7 May, 2002), pointed out that justice can be served when defendants are acquitted because the jury is not satisfied of guilt beyond reasonable doubt. The police persevered with the investigation and in 2006 two brothers were convicted of manslaughter. Vital leads connecting the brothers to the offence were originally missed by investigators and a forensic laboratory, but were later picked up by a private science laboratory.

Victims of crime may also seek justice through the civil system. For example, all criminal assaults are also actionable torts, and victims can thus seek compensation from the attacker. In most cases, there is little point as the defendant does not have sufficient assets, but the mechanism did work in *A v Hoare and Others* (2008). In 1989, the defendant was convicted of raping the claimant and received a life sentence. In 2004, having been released on licence, he won £7 million on the National Lottery. The House of Lords held that, in the circumstances, the claimant's action for damages was not barred by the **Limitation Act 1980**.

When a defendant has been acquitted, victims can bring an action in the civil courts.

The standard of proof is lower in civil courts and it is easier to prove something on a balance of probabilities. An example is the decision of the High Court in December 2005 in which property baron Nicholas van Hoogstraten was held responsible for the murder of a business rival. Sometimes such a civil ruling prompts a new investigation, resulting in a successful criminal prosecution. An example is the Lynn Siddons case. In 1991, the High Court ruled that Michael Brookes had killed the 16-year-old in 1978. The original police case was found to have been bungled and a fresh investigation took place. In 1996, he was convicted of the murder.

Substantive criminal law: the defence of provocation

The aim of the partial defences of provocation and diminished responsibility is to provide substantive justice, whereby those who kill but are not fully responsible for their actions are not found guilty of murder. A conviction for voluntary manslaughter is substituted. The problem with the provocation defence is the requirement set out in *R* v *Duffy* (1949) for a 'sudden and temporary loss of self control'. The general impartial application of this defence results in injustice to women who, by virtue of their comparative strength with their husbands, are less likely to act spontaneously and be able to rely on the strict interpretation of the defence. This has been mitigated to a certain extent by *R* v *Ahluwalia* (1992), in which battered woman syndrome was regarded as evidence of the 'abnormality of mind' required under the defence of diminished responsibility. Clearly, reform of these defences is required before they can be regarded as substantially just. The Ahluwalia decision in effect typecasts battered women as mentally impaired, having to rely on the defence of diminished responsibility, unlike apparently legally sane males who may rely on the provocation defence.

Substantive criminal law: intoxication

This defence is useful in the context of justice because it illustrates the difficulty the law has in striking a balance which is fair to both victim and defendant. Currently, involuntary intoxication is a defence to specific but not basic intent crimes. Formal justice requires consistency in the way rules operate and yet we treat basic and specific intent in different ways. Furthermore, there is potential injustice in that someone can be found guilty even though he or she is clearly unable to form the *mens rea* for even a basic intent crime.

This problem was recognised by the House of Lords in *DPP* v *Majewski* (1977), but it firmly resisted the idea that voluntary intoxication should become a general defence, because this would be socially undesirable. Lord Salmon argued that one important aspect of individual liberty was protection against physical violence, and because the intoxication rule helped to achieve this 'the rule works without imperilling justice'.

Substantive law: tort

It is useful to consider the strict liability torts of nuisance and *Rylands* v *Fletcher* (1868) and the principle of vicarious liability — arguably unjust because they impose liability without blameworthiness. The circumstances in which a duty of care is owed in negligence can also be explored. One requirement is that it must be fair, just and reasonable to impose a duty. Elements of substantial and formal justice were clearly influential in the decision of *Hill* v *Chief Constable of South Yorkshire* (1991).

Elements of distributive and substantive justice can also be seen in the decision in *Donoghue* v *Stevenson* (1932), in which it was held that a duty of care is owed by the manufacturer to the consumer; and it can be argued that to impose a duty of care on someone who is doing his or her best, as in *Nettleship* v *Weston* (1971) and as required under the principle of *Bolam* (1957), is unjust.

Substantive law: contract

The policy underpinning contract law has increasingly moved away from laissez-faire towards protection of the weaker party. This can be seen through the development of consumer laws by the European Union, national legislation and case law. These laws aim to provide substantive justice and also distributive justice in that rights are given to the weaker party.

There is a wealth of illustrative material that can be used, including the law relating to unfair contract terms and implied terms. Further protection is provided by other legislation including the **Consumer Protection from Unfair Trading Regulations 2008** and the **Cancellation of Contracts made in the Consumer's Home or Place of Work etc. Regulations 2008**.

The role of equity in contracts is relevant to the extent to which justice is achieved. The equitable remedies of specific performance and promissory estoppel were introduced to provide justice where the common law failed to do so.

Conclusion

It is clear that there are aspects of English law where the requirement for formal justice has not been met. This is also true of substantive justice, although arguably less so. However, a balanced view would point out that legislative reform such as the **Human Rights Act 1998** and the **Access to Justice Act 1999** have helped to ensure that procedures are more fair and individuals more likely to experience justice. Arguably, substantive justice does underpin the English legal system, and in the miscarriage of justice cases, for example, it was not the substantive law that was in question but the manner in which it was being administered.

It remains true, of course, that substantive law can be changed through enactment, so that laws regarded as unjust can be repealed. It is not so simple to alter the behaviour of those administering the legal system, making formal justice more difficult to achieve.

Judicial creativity

Tip

It is important to be able to address the *extent* to which judges are able to display creativity in the operation of the system of judicial precedent. Some mechanisms of precedent aid judicial creativity and some impede it, and in some areas of law, these mechanisms have been operational in either developing or restricting the development of the law.

Characteristics of the doctrine of precedent which limit judicial creativity

Requirement to follow previous decisions

The doctrine of precedent is based on the idea of *stare decisis*, which means to stand by what has been decided. The courts are bound to follow the decisions made in earlier cases. The doctrine of precedent operates within a hierarchical court structure, with the lower courts being bound by the precedents made in the higher courts. The binding part of the judgement is called the *ratio decidendi*, meaning the legal reason for the decision.

Lord Denning campaigned for many years to free the Court of Appeal from being bound by its own decisions and by the House of Lords, in order to allow greater flexibility. The essence of his argument was that once a precedent is set by the House of Lords, only the House of Lords can change it, yet most cases never reach the House of Lords. During his campaign, Lord Denning refused to follow binding decisions of both the Court of Appeal and the House of Lords. While generally agreeing with the principles of his decisions, he was usually rebuked by the Law Lords for disregarding the rules. On one occasion, Lord Cross said: 'It is not for any inferior court — be it a County Court or a division of the Court of Appeal presided over by Lord Denning — to review the decisions of this House. Such a review can only be undertaken by this House itself under the declaration of 1966.'

Judges are dependent on cases being brought before the courts

Judges are dependent on cases being brought before them in the higher courts for the opportunity to create law. For example, judges had felt since the 1960s that the old rule of a builder not owing a duty in tort to the person to whom he sold a property was unfair. In *Dutton* v *Bognor Regis UDC* (1972), Lord Denning said *in obiter* that the builder should owe a duty of care, but the opportunity to follow this persuasive precedent did not arise until 1978 in *Batty* v *Metropolitan Property Realisations Ltd*.

Characteristics of the doctrine of precedent which aid judicial creativity

Practice Statement

Under the 1966 Practice Statement, the House of Lords has the power to depart from its previous decisions when it appears 'right to do so'. The Law Lords have used this power sparingly because of an overall desire to achieve certainty in the law.

However, despite the limitations set out in the Practice Statement and the self-imposed restraint which has characterised the Law Lords in a majority of cases heard since 1966, it has been used to bring about significant changes in the law. Notable examples are that occupiers have some duty in respect of trespassers, *British Railways Board* v *Herrington* (1972); that no participant can use duress as a defence to a murder charge, *R* v *Howe* (1987); that *Hansard* can in certain circumstances be referred to when interpreting a statute, *Pepper* v *Hart* (1993); and that the *mens rea* of recklessness should always be subjective, *R* v *G* (2004).

Overruling

Higher courts can always overrule earlier precedents set in lower courts. Overruling must not be confused with reversing, which involves a higher court changing the outcome of a case on appeal.

Distinguishing

Judges in all courts may avoid following a precedent by finding that the facts of the case before them are materially different from those of the case in which the binding precedent was set. In *Balfour* v *Balfour* (1919), Mrs Balfour was unable to enforce a maintenance agreement made with her husband. The *ratio decidendi* of the case was that there is no intention to create legal relations when agreements are made within marriage. In *Merritt* v *Merritt* (1970), the defendant husband sought to rely on the Balfour principle to avoid honouring an agreement he had made with his estranged wife. The court distinguished the case on the material difference that the agreement, albeit made within marriage, had been made after the couple had separated. The decision limited the scope of the Balfour principle and created a new rule in respect of separated couples.

Dissenting judgements

Judges in the higher courts may disagree with the legal principles being applied in cases before them. In such cases, they may deliver a dissenting judgement, in which they outline principles they believe should apply. Dissenting judgements are persuasive precedents and so may be followed in future cases. Some key areas of law have developed from such judgements. The law on negligent misstatement was developed from the dissenting judgement of Lord Denning in *Candler* v *Crane Christmas* (1951). The majority judges held that accountants, who prepared a company's accounts knowing that they would be relied upon by third parties, owed no duty of care. Lord Denning, however, stipulated the circumstances in which such a duty should be owed. His judgement formed the basis of the decision in *Hedley Byrne* v *Heller* (1964), in which it was held that, had there not been a disclaimer, the claimants could have recovered compensation for economic loss caused by a negligent misstatement. The circumstances outlined in *Caparo* v *Dickman* (1990) for when such a duty should be owed are very similar to those originally outlined by Lord Denning.

Other persuasive precedents

When delivering their judgements, judges sometimes speculate on what their decision would have been had the facts been slightly different. These *obiter* statements are persuasive and may become the *ratio decidendi* of future cases. In *R* v *Brown* (1993) the defendants, who had engaged in sadomasochistic activities, were unable to rely on the defence of consent when prosecuted under the **Offences Against the Person Act 1861**. However, the Lords stated *in obiter* that consent could be a defence to painful practices such as tattooing and piercing. In *R* v *Wilson* (1996), the defendant husband was able to rely on this defence when he used a hot knife to brand his initials onto his wife's buttocks at her request. The Court of Appeal held that the defendant was engaged in body decoration, which was similar to body piercing or tattooing.

Other examples include *R* v *R* (1991), where the House of Lords was influenced by Court of Appeal arguments on the issue of rape within marriage, and *Attorney General for Jersey* v *Holley* (2005), in which the Privy Council was influential in developing the defence of provocation, in spite of conflicting House of Lords authority.

The Court of Appeal

In practice, the Court of Appeal makes a great deal of new law. A good example is *R* v *Woollin* (1998), which clarified the law on oblique intent and has become the leading judgement, despite several earlier House of Lords decisions. It was also the Court of Appeal in *R* v *Prentice* (1994) that effectively reintroduced gross negligence manslaughter into the modern law.

> **Tip**
>
> Evidence of the ability of judges to be creative and develop the law, despite the constraints of precedent, is provided by the fact that in a number of significant areas of law, almost all the rules are judge-made. This presents an opportunity to refer to areas of substantive law in detail. For example, in criminal law, the rules on the *mens rea* of murder, on involuntary manslaughter and on defences such as intoxication and self-defence may be considered. In contract law, examples include the rules on formation and discharge of contracts. In tort, candidates could refer to areas such as the rules relating to nervous shock or economic loss, private nuisance and the rule in

Rylands v *Fletcher*. Another area of tort that judges have begun to develop is invasion of privacy. In actions brought under Article 8 of the European Convention on Human Rights — the right to respect for private and family life — a number of celebrities have successfully claimed against newspapers that have published photographs of them in their private life without consent. Cases include *Murray* v *Express Newspapers and Another* (2008) brought by the author J. K. Rowling and her husband, and *Mosley* v *News Group Newspapers Ltd* (2008), in which the Formula One boss successfully sued the *News of the World* in respect of an article headed 'F1 boss has sick Nazi orgy with 5 hookers'.

The extent to which judges display creativity in statutory interpretation

The literal rule

Supporters of the literal rule argue that judges should apply statutes as written in all circumstances. Judges who follow the literal rule are not creative and do not develop the law, even when common sense demands it. An example is *Fisher* v *Bell* (1961). A shopkeeper was charged under the **Offensive Weapons Act 1959** for offering for sale an offensive weapon. He had displayed flick knives in the shop window. The court held that no offence had been committed as, according to contract law, what he had done amounted to an invitation to treat and not to an offer.

The mischief rule

When interpreting a statute, judges may be creative in that they broaden or narrow its application. This is particularly relevant in terms of the mischief and purposive approaches. The mischief rule requires judges to look back to the law before the Act in question was made in order to determine the gap in the law that the Act was intended to remedy. In *Smith* v *Hughes* (1960), a prostitute was prosecuted under the **Street Offences Act 1958** for soliciting in the street. She had attracted the attention of men who were in the street by tapping on her first-floor window. The court held, using the mischief approach, that the mischief the Act had been passed to prevent was men in the street being accosted by prostitutes, and that therefore she was guilty. The Act was thus made broader in application because it was not limited to situations where the prostitute was in the street itself.

A further example is *Royal College of Nursing* v *DHSS* (1981), in which the House of Lords had to decide how the **Abortion Act 1967** should be interpreted. The Act stated that lawful abortion requires that a pregnancy 'is terminated by a registered medical practitioner'. In 1967, the method of producing an abortion was surgical and so would have needed to be performed by a doctor. However, by the 1980s abortions were being induced by drip-feeding a drug which caused the fetus to be discharged from the uterus. This was performed by midwives and nurses. The House of Lords held that the mischief the Act had been passed to prevent was illegal, backstreet abortion, and that therefore it was legal for midwives and nurses to administer the drug.

The purposive approach

The purposive approach to legislation has become increasingly popular among English judges, particularly since the UK joined the European Union, because EU law is stated in general principles that can be applied to a broad range of circumstances and it is important that English judges take a purposive approach to interpreting Acts of Parliament which have been passed to comply with European obligations.

Lord Denning, in *Bulmer* v *Bollinger* (1974), pointed out that when interpreting such legislation, English courts must depart from the traditional methods of interpreting domestic statutes and follow the European pattern.

The European Convention on Human Rights is similarly set out in broad terms. The judges in the European Court of Human Rights therefore also use the purposive approach. The **Human Rights Act 1998** requires that all legislation be interpreted so that, as far as possible, it is compatible with the convention. This will inevitably result in English judges increasingly using the purposive approach.

Following the House of Lords' decision in *Pepper* v *Hart* (1993), judges may now make reference to *Hansard* in limited circumstances, as an aid to interpretation. It is arguable that this decision was brought about by the shift in favour from the literal to the purposive approach and it has certainly facilitated the latter approach.

The balance between the roles of Parliament and the judiciary

The constitutional position

Constitutionally, it is the role of Parliament to create law and, as Lord Radcliffe said, 'it is unacceptable constitutionally that there should be two sources of law-making at work at the same time'. The basis of the constitutional position is that Parliament is democratically elected (at least, the House of Commons is) and that the legislative programme should to some extent be influenced by the electorate. Judges, on the other hand, are not elected.

The constitutional role of judges has changed in recent years through the UK's membership of the European Union. Section 2(4) of the **European Communities Act 1972** states that European Community law should take precedence over English law. In giving effect to this section, English judges have been able to exercise powers that were not available to them in the past. For example, in *R* v *Secretary of State for Transport ex parte Factortame* (1990), the European Court of Justice held that domestic courts are entitled to ignore provisions of domestic legislation which are in conflict with provisions of directly enforceable European law. In this case it was also held that domestic courts could suspend domestic legislation while awaiting a decision of the European Court of Justice.

The **Human Rights Act 1998** has also significantly altered the balance between the judges and Parliament. Section 3 requires legislation to be interpreted so that, as far as possible, it is compatible with the European Convention on Human Rights. This was demonstrated in *A and others* v *Secretary of State for the Home Department* (2004). The House of Lords held that s.23 of the **Anti-Terrorism, Crime and Security Act 2001**, in permitting the detention of suspected international terrorists indefinitely without charge or trial, was incompatible with Articles 5 and 14 of the European Convention on Human Rights.

Policy

Formulation of policy is the role of Parliament. Policy is a set of ideas about what should be done and sets out objectives and intended directions of change. Ronald Dworkin made a distinction between rules and principles on the one hand and policies on the other. A policy, he said, is a standard setting out of a goal to be achieved, usually in terms of the economic, social or political well-being of the community. A principle, on the other hand, sets individual rights above communal well-being and imposes a standard of justice or fairness or some other moral dimension. Matters of policy should be left to the elected legislators; judges should concern themselves only with legal principles.

However, judges are sometimes placed in positions where they have to make policy decisions. First, judges have a role in judicial review and as guardians of individual rights. By giving priority to individual rights over policy, and thereby ruling against the government, they will be making decisions which could be seen as being political and which have an impact on policy goals. For example, the House of Lords' decision in *A and others* v *Secretary of State for the Home Department* (December 2004) had an impact on how the government deals with terrorism.

The second problem for judges is that they sometimes have to make controversial decisions, which will inevitably have policy implications. In *Gillick* v *West Norfolk and Wisbech Area Health Authority* (1986), the issue for the judges to decide was whether or not girls under the age of 16 should be prescribed contraceptives without parental consent. The House of Lords held that a girl under 16 could be prescribed contraceptives without parental consent only if she fully understood the issues involved. Abortions carried out on girls under 16 without parental consent raises a similar issue.

Policy in statutory interpretation

Judges who favour the literal rule usually justify it on the grounds that they should not change the wording of statutes, because to do so would be to usurp the legislative function and that is not their role. If the outcome of a judicial decision is unsatisfactory, the proper solution is for Parliament to make the legislative change.

Judges adopted this approach in *In the Estate of Bravda* (1968), where the Court of Appeal had to deal with an unfortunate situation under the **Wills Act 1837**. The Act clearly stated that any beneficiary who signed a will automatically lost his or her right to benefit under the will. In this case, a man's daughters were the main beneficiaries, and the Court felt that it would be right to ensure that where there are two independent witnesses, the mere fact that a beneficiary has signed as a witness should not operate (as it then did) to defeat the intentions of the testator. However, rather than adopt either the golden or mischief rule and change the wording of the Act, the Court felt that, as a policy issue, the change should be made by Parliament. **The Wills Acts 1968** was passed to make the necessary changes.

On the other hand, there are examples of decisions in statutory interpretation which are based on policy. In *Re Sigsworth* (1935), the Court, using the golden rule, held that a man who murdered his mother, who had died intestate, should not benefit from his crime. It was contrary to public policy to allow such an undesirable outcome.

In the case of *Royal College of Nursing* v *DHSS* (1981), the majority in the House of Lords was influenced by what it considered to be the policy of the **Abortion Act 1967**, namely broadening of the grounds of lawful abortion and ensuring that it was carried out with proper skill. The two dissenting judges, Lords Wilberforce and Edmund-Davies, argued that the Act should not be rewritten because it dealt with 'a controversial subject involving moral or social judgements on which opinions strongly differ'. In other words, this was a policy issue, which should be left to Parliament.

Professor Griffith has argued that where there is ambiguity in a statute, the judges choose the interpretation which best suits their view of what policy should be. An example that supports this argument is *Bromley LBC* v *GLC* (1983). Griffith claimed that what the House of Lords was doing in this case was making a choice between two interpretations, based not on what Parliament intended, but primarily on 'the Law Lords' strong preference for the principles of the market economy with a dislike of heavy subsidisation for social purposes'.

Policy in criminal law

Intoxication
In *DPP* v *Majewski* (1977), policy issues were clearly the basis of the decision. Majewski, after drinking alcohol and taking drugs, attacked people in a public house and then the police officers who tried to arrest him. The House of Lords refused to accept the defence of voluntary intoxication on policy grounds. One of the prime purposes of the criminal law is to protect people from violence and to allow voluntary intoxication as a defence would leave the citizen unprotected. Lord Salmon said: 'If there were to be no penal sanction for any injury unlawfully inflicted under the complete mastery of drink or drugs, voluntarily taken, the social consequences would be appalling.'

Provocation

In *R* v *Ahluwalia* (1992), where the defendant had clearly not acted in the heat of the moment, it was held that important considerations of public policy would be involved should provocation be redefined so as to blur the distinction between sudden loss of self-control and deliberate retribution. The court was not willing to consider such a change.

Consent to the infliction of violence

It has long been recognised that to take part in sporting activities is to consent to the possible infliction of some degree of injury. In the case of boxing, for example, some injury is almost inevitable. In *R* v *Wilson* (1996), there is the acceptance that within marriage, consent can be given to the infliction of injury, yet in *R* v *Brown* (1994), consenting adults were found guilty. Reading the judgements of the House of Lords, it is clear that they were using policy considerations. For example, Lord Templeman expressed the view that 'society was entitled to protect itself against a cult of violence. Pleasure derived from the infliction of pain was an evil thing. Cruelty was uncivilised'.

Policy in tort

The extension of negligence into ever more diverse areas has also led to policy issues being raised. Decisions are justified by reference to wider social or economic considerations rather than to precedent or to legal principles. This is apparent in the law relating to pure economic loss. In *Spartan Steel and Alloys Ltd* v *Martin & Co Ltd* (1973), Lord Denning openly based his leading judgement on policy. He said:

> At bottom I think the question of recovering economic loss is one of policy. Whenever the courts draw a line to mark out the bounds of duty, they do it as a matter of policy so as to limit the responsibility of the defendant. Whenever the courts set bounds to the damages recoverable — saying that they are, or are not, too remote — they do it as a matter of policy so as to limit the liability of the defendant.

Similar policy issues have influenced the development of the law relating to nervous shock. In *Alcock* v *Chief Constable of South Yorkshire* (1992), Lord Oliver openly used the word 'policy' in explaining his decision to limit the range of potential victims to whom a duty of care could be owed.

Should judges create law?

Tip

An exam question may ask whether judges should make law. This requires consideration of the benefits and the problems posed by judicial law-making. It is also useful to consider the views of the judges themselves. Stronger candidates will be able to draw on a wide range of arguments and provide illustration.

Benefits of judicial law-making

Flexibility

It takes many months for an Act of Parliament to be passed. One of the advantages of the common law system is that the law is able to respond to new situations. Within the limits set by precedent and the rules of statutory interpretation, judges are able to develop the law in ways that reflect changing social and technological circumstances. For example, the law has been adapted to deal with the effect of life support systems on the exact point of death, *R v Malcherek and Steel* (1981); and technical developments in the way abortions are carried out, *Royal College of Nursing* v *DHSS* (1981).

In contract law, the postal rule has been adapted to deal with instantaneous forms of communication, *Entores* v *Miles Far East* (1955).

In the law of tort, the House of Lords extended the law on nervous shock to cover situations where the secondary victim came upon the 'immediate aftermath', *McLoughlin* v *O'Brian* (1982).

Insufficient parliamentary time

The government will be intent on pushing through a legislative programme that fulfils its political goals. Furthermore, in contrast to judges who have only one case before them at any one time, MPs and peers have many conflicting priorities to attend to. Consequently, non-controversial, politically insignificant reforms to the law are often left aside for many years. For example, despite the work of the Law Commission, the law on non-fatal offences remains unreformed. Similarly, moral issues are often not included in the legislative programme and the judiciary is consequently left to determine whether development of the law is required. This was clearly the case with husband rape. It had long been regarded by society as unacceptable, but successive parliaments had not found time for statutory change. The long-awaited decision was made in *R* v *R* (1991).

Law made by lawyers/experts

Judges are legal experts and thus better equipped to develop the law than Parliament. Because they are trained to apply existing principles and relate developments to the existing law, the law is more likely to remain consistent and coherent.

Problems with judicial law-making

Constitutional position

The constitutional position is that Parliament creates law and the judges apply it. Formulation of policy is the role of a democratically elected parliament which will recognise the will of the electorate. Judges are unelected. In addition, they are arguably not representative of the population. Judges are drawn from a narrow social group and this raises the possibility, identified by Professor Griffith, that they will inevitably have views which reflect this narrow social background. Women and people from ethnic minorities are under-represented, especially amongst the senior judiciary. For example, until the appointment of Lady Hale in January 2004 there were no female Law Lords.

Lack of research

When Parliament wants to introduce a new piece of legislation, there is considerable opportunity for comprehensive research. Very often, legislation will be the result of recommendations from the Law Reform bodies, which possess the expertise to research an area thoroughly. The Law Commission is a permanent law reform body and has had considerable success in having recommendations recognised in Acts of Parliament. Examples of such legislation include the **Contracts (Rights of Third Parties) Act 1999** and the **Computer Misuse Act 1990**. The Green Paper stage allows for interested parties to be consulted and the passage of the bill through Parliament will involve many debates among people who are able to research the relevant issues. Judges' decisions, however, will be based on the evidence presented to them by the parties involved in the case. They cannot consider arguments about the general social, economic or moral aspects, even though their decision, as in *Gillick* v *West Norfolk and Wisbech Area Health Authority* (1986) for example, may inevitably have implications for society generally.

Judge-made law operates retrospectively

Judge-made law applies to events that have taken place prior to its creation.

It is useful to consider the decision in *R* v *R* (1991), the effect of which was to turn an act, which was lawful at the time it was committed, into a serious criminal offence. The decision was upheld by the European Court of Human Rights. In *SW and CR* v *United Kingdom* (1995), the ECtHR held that the UK had not been in breach of Article 7 of the Convention, which states that no one should be found guilty of an offence which was not an offence at the time it was committed. The Court's reasoning was that judicial law-making was well entrenched in legal tradition and the development of the law in this case had been reasonably foreseeable.

The reasoning of the ECtHR was followed by the Court of Appeal in *R* v *Crooks* (2004). The defendant had forced his wife to have sexual intercourse without her consent in 1970, 32 years before his conviction and 21 years before the *R* v *R* decision. Upholding the rape conviction, Judge LJ said that the defendant should have foreseen that the marital exemption was about to be removed. The right of the wife to freedom from inhuman or degrading treatment outweighed the defendant's right not to be tried retrospectively.

Legislation, however, usually operates prospectively, taking effect on a fixed date after the Act has received royal assent. This allows people time to prepare for the change in the law.

This problem does not arise with legislation, which operates prospectively. It is usually the case that legislation comes into effect on a fixed date after the Act has received the Royal Assent, in order to allow time for people to prepare for the law change.

In some countries, including the United States, cases only apply prospectively. This concept has been considered in relation to the English legal system. In a speech in 1987, the then Lord Chancellor, Lord Mackay, discussed the possibility of allowing prospective overruling, whereby the court might uphold the existing precedent in the instant case but declare it overruled for the future. The main problem with this idea is that most litigants would find it hard to accept that they had won their case only for future litigants, not for themselves. There would seem little point in going to court at all.

Judge-made law is incremental in nature

Judges can only make law on the facts of the case before them. They cannot lay down a comprehensive code to cover all similar situations. Some areas of law, for example negligence, might be well suited to this case-by-case approach. However, with other areas it is not helpful when one small change is made, such as the introduction of gross negligence manslaughter in *R v Prentice* (1994) and *R v Adomako* (1995), when really the whole area of involuntary manslaughter needs to be properly reformed.

Judge-made law thus develops in an unstructured, random way. It is dependent on cases being brought and then appealed through to a court sufficiently senior to make a new precedent.

Complexity/technical distinctions

One of the arguments often used against precedent as a law-making process is that judges make technical distinctions between the case they are deciding and the precedent, in order to avoid following the precedent. The result of this is that the law becomes complex and confusing, with many minor technical distinctions.

Judicial preference

Judicial views on the constitutional position

There are contrasting views among judges on the extent to which they should be making new rules of law. Lord Justice Oliver argued that for judges to develop new concepts of law would be an abandonment by the court of its proper function and an assumption by it of the mantle of legislator. This view originally prevailed in the Debbie Purdy case. The decision of the High Court, upheld by the Court of Appeal, was justified by Lord Justice Scott Baker, who said: 'The offence of assisted suicide is very widely drawn to cover all manner of different circumstances, only Parliament can change it.' However, this ruling was overturned by the House of Lords in July 2009 (see p. 12).

Lord Scarman, by contrast, put forward the view in *McLoughlin v O'Brian* (1982) that the court's proper function was to adjudicate according to principle. If principle led to results which were felt to be socially unacceptable, then Parliament could legislate to overrule them. The real risk to the common law would be if it stood still, halted by a conservative judicial approach.

Judicial law-making is more acceptable in some areas of law than others

Some judges argue that the role of the judiciary should be determined by the type of law involved. The view of Lord Reid in the 1960s was that judges should not so readily create new law in areas such as property, contract, family and criminal law, where certainty is of vital importance, but that they could have more freedom to do so in the areas of tort and public and administrative law, where the judges regard their creative role as legitimate and appropriate.

Lord Devlin argued that judges should stick to activist law-making, by which he meant developing the law in line with the consensus view of society, and avoid dynamic law-making, which involved taking sides on controversial issues.

However, judges cannot avoid making decisions in controversial cases. These might be cases which are politically sensitive, such as *Bromley LBC* v *GLC* (1983) and *ex parte Pinochet* (2000), or ones which raise profound moral or social issues, for example *Gillick* v *West Norfolk and Wisbech Area Health Authority* (1986) and *Airedale NHS Trust* v *Bland* (1993). In practice, judges have to get involved in controversial areas because such cases are brought before the courts. It is difficult to see how, in deciding any of these cases, judges could have avoided engaging in dynamic law-making and offending at least one section of the community.

Personal preference

Judges adopt contrasting views on their role and it is difficult to escape the conclusion that the view they take is largely a matter of personal preference. Lord Denning, in particular, had a crusading approach to judicial law-making and he was determined not to be fettered by existing legal rules. He argued that it was the duty of judges to do justice and not to follow unjust precedents or restrictive approaches to statutory interpretation. But he was firmly opposed by senior Law Lords, including Viscount Simmonds, who described his approach to statutory interpretation of 'filling in the gaps' as a 'naked usurpation of the legislative function'. David Robertson, writing in 1998, concluded: 'Law in almost any case that comes before the Lords turns out to be whatever their Lordships feel it ought to be.'

Conclusion

It is evident that, in some respects, Parliament is more suited than the judiciary to develop the law. However, areas of the law which are largely judge-made seem to work just as well as those made almost exclusively by Parliament. Through the doctrine of precedent and their role in statutory interpretation, judges frequently have to develop the law by clarifying, and in some cases putting right, what is written in an Act of Parliament.

Fault

The meaning of 'fault'

There are various definitions of 'fault'. The *Concise Oxford Dictionary* provides many: 'defect, imperfection, blemish, of character...thing wrongly done...responsibility for something wrong...blame'. The *Collins Concise Dictionary* provides similar definitions: 'responsibility for a mistake or misdeed...guilty of error, culpable...blame'.

While there are various definitions of fault, perhaps the core meaning is 'responsibility'. The definition, 'responsibility for something wrong', would appear to be the most useful for the purposes of discussing the role of fault in English law.

Fault in criminal law

Actus reus

To be found guilty of most criminal offences, an *actus reus* must be present. The *actus reus*, meaning 'prohibited act', is made up of the acts, circumstances and consequences of a specific offence. It comprises the physical elements of the crime. In order to be found guilty of a criminal offence, the accused must commit the *actus reus* voluntarily. If the accused is not in control of his or her own actions, then he or she cannot be said to be acting voluntarily or at fault. There are criminal defences, including automatism and duress, which the accused may plead in such circumstances, proof of which will result in acquittal. The accused will thus not be held responsible for actions which are not the result of his or her rational will.

Automatism arises when someone suffers total loss of control due to external factors. In *R* v *Bailey* (1983) the accused, a diabetic, was charged under s.18 of the **Offences Against the Person Act 1861** after he hit his ex-girlfriend's new boyfriend on the head with an iron bar. He successfully claimed the defence of automatism. He had been in a hypoglycaemic state brought about by a failure to eat after drinking some sugar and water.

Mens rea

The *mens rea* is the mental element of the criminal offence and is usually defined in terms of intention or recklessness. The state of mind required for a conviction varies from one offence to another.

Intention can be either direct, where the purpose of the accused is to bring about the prohibited consequence, or indirect, where the accused recognises the result is a virtual certainty.

Recklessness can be defined as unjustified risk-taking and is now always considered as subjective following the House of Lords judgement in *R* v *G* (2004), which abolished Caldwell recklessness. Subjective recklessness requires the defendant knowingly to take a risk.

Murder and voluntary manslaughter

Murder is the most serious homicide offence. This fact is reflected in the mandatory sentence of life imprisonment. The accused must have had the intention to kill or to cause grievous bodily harm.

Partial defences to murder are contained in the **Homicide Act 1957** and, if proven, allow a conviction for voluntary manslaughter. The partial defences of diminished responsibility and provocation apply to situations where the accused is considered not to be totally in control of what he or she is doing. The defences thus recognise that such defendants are less at fault than murderers and so should be less liable for the consequences of their actions. The less serious nature of voluntary manslaughter is recognised through the life sentence being discretionary rather than mandatory.

Under s.3 of the **Homicide Act 1957**, the defence of provocation requires proof that provocative conduct caused the defendant to lose self-control, and that a reasonable person would have reacted in the same way. One concern about this defence is that a defendant with a level of fault that justifies a murder conviction can claim to be provoked by relatively minor things, such as the crying of a baby (*R* v *Doughty,* 2006). In 2005, the Law Commission recommended that the defence should require 'gross' provocation, meaning the defendant would have to have a 'justifiable sense of being seriously wronged'.

Involuntary manslaughter

Involuntary manslaughter is much more difficult to classify in terms of fault. Now that the definition of recklessness is clearly subjective, following *R* v *G* (2004), it is hard to see how the objective test in the definition of 'dangerous' in unlawful and dangerous act manslaughter can be justified. The definition of 'dangerous' is that given in *R* v *Church* (1967) as meaning 'in the sense that a sober and reasonable person would inevitably recognise that it carried some risk of harm'.

Gross negligence manslaughter was reintroduced into English law by the House of Lords in *R* v *Adomako* (1995). The decision was in line with the actions of the Court of Appeal decision in *R* v *Prentice* (1994). The *mens rea* for the offence was gross negligence, which is not fully defined. Lord Mackay in *R* v *Adomako* (1995) was unwilling to provide a detailed definition of gross negligence. However, he quoted Lord Hewart CJ, who in *R* v *Bateman* (1925) stated that it was 'such disregard for the life and safety of others as to amount to a crime against the State and conduct deserving punishment'.

The problem with this definition is that it is far too broad and leaves up to the jury the decision as to what amounts to gross negligence in each case. In *R* v *Misra and Srivas-*

tava (2004), the Court of Appeal held that there must be a risk of death, and that risk of bodily injury or injury to health is not sufficient.

Both types of involuntary manslaughter therefore have significant objective elements, and thus seem to be out of step with most other important areas of criminal law. The rules have been criticised by the Law Commission as unsatisfactory.

Non-fatal offences

The operation of fault in non-fatal offences is also inconsistent. It is clear that all of the offences require proof of fault for a conviction. However, while some of the offences have a *mens rea* requirement which equates with the harm caused, others do not.

According to s.18 of the **Offences Against the Person Act 1861**, assault and battery require intention or subjective recklessness to bring about the prohibited result of the *actus reus*. However, sections 47 and 20 both require intention or recklessness to bring about a result less serious than that specified in the *actus reus*. If charged with a s.47 offence, the accused can be found guilty of causing actual bodily harm, despite having only the intention or subjective recklessness to cause an assault or battery. Under s.20, a conviction can be sustained for wounding or causing grievous bodily harm when the accused only intended or took the risk of causing some harm. Under sections 47 and 20, the accused is thus held legally responsible for a level of harm higher than that he or she is at fault in bringing about.

The distinction between legal fault and motive

In criminal law, the legal fault requirement is stipulated in the definition of the offences. However, criminal law takes no account of motive. This is illustrated clearly by the issue of mercy killings. People who perpetrate mercy killings do so out of care for the victim and often with the best possible motive, but they will still be technically guilty of murder.

In *R* v *Cox* (1992), Dr Cox was found guilty of attempted murder. He had injected a terminally ill, elderly patient who was suffering constant severe pain, with a lethal drug, after the patient asked him to end her suffering. Where possible, the judge may take account of motive when sentencing, and Dr Cox was given a suspended prison sentence.

In *ex parte Diane Pretty* (2001) the House of Lords held that the husband of a motor neurone disease sufferer could be subject to a criminal prosecution if he helped his wife end her life.

Strict liability offences

There are many crimes for which there is no fault requirement in terms of *mens rea*. This is a significant departure from the principle that to be guilty of a criminal offence a defendant should be proved to be at fault.

Strict liability offences are generally regulatory offences, concerned with public safety, and usually made by statute. They cover situations such as minor road traffic offences, food safety laws, protection of the environment, and the sale of alcohol and tobacco to underage children.

In *Harrow LBC* v *Shah* (1999), the defendant, a newsagent, was convicted of selling a lottery ticket to a 13-year-old. The fact that he had told staff not to sell lottery tickets to under-16s, had put up a notice in the shop to this effect, and had told staff to ask for proof of identity was irrelevant.

The courts are reluctant, in the absence of express statutory permission, to impose strict liability for offences that are truly criminal in nature. In such situations there is a presumption that *mens rea* is required. This principle is illustrated in cases such as *B* v *DPP* (2000).

While strict liability offences do not require *mens rea*, they do require an *actus reus*. The *actus reus* must be committed voluntarily, so it would appear that even strict liability offences are dependent on proof of fault, albeit to a lesser extent.

Absolute liability offences

Absolute liability offences, sometimes referred to as 'state of affairs' offences, are those that do not require *mens rea* and do not require the act to be carried out voluntarily. In *Winzar* v *Chief Constable of Kent* (1983), the accused was charged with being found drunk on the highway. He had entered a hospital while drunk and had been asked to leave. When he refused, the police were called. The police forcefully removed him from the hospital to their car, which was parked on the highway. He was convicted, despite having been forced by the police to commit the offence.

Mandatory sentences

Mandatory sentences for murder under the **Crime (Sentencing) Act 1997** would also appear to go against the principle that decisions in criminal law should be based on the amount of fault displayed by the defendant. The mandatory life sentence for murder has been widely criticised, particularly in the context of 'mercy killing' cases such as *R* v *Cox* (1992), and in 1989 a House of Lords select committee recommended its abolition. The 1997 Act has been challenged under the **Human Rights Act 1998**. It imposes automatic sentences for subsequent offences. These automatic sentences can only be avoided in 'exceptional' circumstances. In *R* v *Offen* (2001), in order to prevent a possible breach of Articles 3 or 5, the Court of Appeal interpreted 'exceptional' to mean any case where there was not a danger to the public, thus significantly weakening the scope of the Act to impose automatic sentences for subsequent offences.

Despite the criticism of mandatory sentences, they have been retained by subsequent legislation. For example, s.225 of the **Criminal Justice Act 2003** imposes an automatic life sentence if a person is convicted of a second serious violent or sexual offence.

Fault in the law of tort

Negligence

For a claimant to succeed in an action of negligence, three elements must be proved: duty of care, breach and causation. In deciding whether there has been a breach of duty, the courts consider whether the 'reasonable man' would have behaved as the defendant did. A defendant not behaving as the 'reasonable man' would be seen to have been at fault.

In *Bolton* v *Stone* (1951), the claimant had been hit by a cricket ball. The court considered the likelihood of the risk of injury to be very small on the basis that balls had flown out of the cricket ground between six and ten times in 30 years. The court decided that the 'reasonable man' would have acted the same way and would not have taken further preventative measures.

Occupiers' liability

Occupiers' liability is also based on the notion of reasonableness. The **Occupiers' Liability Acts 1957** and **1984** make occupiers responsible for the safety of visitors and non-visitors respectively while on their premises. An occupier fulfils the duty owed by taking reasonable precautions. In *Martin* v *Middlesbrough Corporation* (1965), the council was held liable to the child claimant who slipped in a playground and cut herself on a broken glass bottle. The council did not have adequate arrangements in place for the disposal of such litter. However, in *Sawyer* v *Simonds* (1966), the defendants were not liable when a customer fell and injured himself on broken glass while in their pub. They had made arrangements for the bar to be checked every 20 minutes and this was considered by the court to be reasonable.

Under s.2(2)(b), people on the premises in the exercise of their calling are owed a lower duty of care, since they are expected to know what they are doing. There is a shift in responsibility from the occupier to the visitor. In *Roles* v *Nathan* (1963), chimney sweeps had been hired to clean central heating flues. They were warned of danger from fumes but entered the chimney and died. The occupiers were not liable since they were not at fault. The sweeps were acting in the exercise of their calling, so it was their responsibility to know about the dangers.

An occupier is considered to be less at fault if a trespasser is injured than if the victim is a lawful visitor. This is reflected in the **Occupiers' Liability Act 1984**, which limits the duty owed to trespassers to the following circumstances:
- the occupier is aware that a danger exists
- the occupier is aware that the trespasser is in the vicinity of the danger
- the danger is of a kind that the occupier should guard against in all circumstances

While the courts are more sympathetic to child trespassers, the courts' reluctance to impose liability in respect of trespassers is evident from cases such as *Tomlinson* v *Congleton BC* (2003). The unsuccessful claimant, aged 18, dived into a lake in a public park and suffered a severe spinal injury. The council had placed warning signs and was planning to make the lake inaccessible to the public when the accident occurred.

Fault of the victim: contributory negligence

In apportioning damages in tort, the law takes into account the fault of the victim. Section 1(1) of the **Law Reform (Contributory Negligence) Act 1945** states that where any person suffers damage as the result partly of his own fault, the damages recoverable shall be reduced to such an extent as the court thinks just and equitable, having regard to the claimant's share in the responsibility for the damage.

In *Froom* v *Butcher* (1976), the claimant's damages were reduced by 25%. He had been involved in a vehicle accident caused by the negligence of the defendant, but was partly responsible for his injuries, as he had not been wearing a seat belt.

Nuisance

While it can be seen that liability in negligence or occupiers' liability depends upon proof of fault, in other areas of the law of tort this is not the case.

Nuisance is not concerned with the fault of the defendant. Whether the defendant took reasonable care to avoid the nuisance or not is irrelevant. Reasonableness in nuisance is concerned with the level of interference with the claimant's enjoyment of his or her land. However, motive or malice of the defendant is an issue. This is illustrated by *Christie* v *Davey* (1893). Whenever the claimant gave music lessons, the defendant deliberately shrieked and banged on the adjoining wall. The claimant succeeded because the defendant had acted maliciously.

Rylands v *Fletcher* (1868)

The rule in *Rylands* v *Fletcher* originally involved strict liability for damage caused by something escaping from the defendant's land. This rule only applied to non-natural or artificial use of land. In this case, the defendants were liable for escape of water into a mine, even though there was no wrongful intent or negligence. The water constituted a non-natural use, due to the non-natural quantity. However, the case of *Cambridge Water Co. Ltd* v *Eastern Counties Leather* (1994) introduced a fault requirement. The House of Lords held that defendants would only be liable for damage of a foreseeable type.

Vicarious liability

The principle of vicarious liability imposes liability for someone else's fault. Under this principle, employers can be held vicariously liable for torts committed by their employees in the course of their employment. No liability will be incurred for acts done which are considered to be outside the course of employment or when the employee is considered to be 'on a frolic of his own'. The principle applies in respect of prohibited acts, and acts which are carried out in a prohibited or unauthorised manner. In *Rose v Plenty* (1976), the claimant, aged 13, was helping the defendant deliver milk. This was forbidden by his employers. The claimant was injured through the defendant's employee's negligent driving. The employers were held liable. The employee was doing what he was employed to do, i.e. deliver milk, but he was doing it in an unauthorised manner. While it may appear unfair on the employer, the principle of vicarious liability is justified on the basis that the act is done for the employer's benefit, and the victim is more likely to be compensated due to the requirement of compulsory insurance.

Liability for defective products

Liability for defective products was dependent upon proof of fault until the **Consumer Protection Act 1987** was introduced. Claimants had to prove that the manufacturer was in breach of his or her duty of care. The 1987 Act imposed what is, in effect, strict liability on producers for damage caused by defective products.

Moves towards a no-fault-based system for accident victims

In more recent years, there has been a move from the laissez-faire ideal which dominated in the nineteenth century. The law has increasingly come to focus on the injured victim rather than the blameworthy individual. Twentieth-century legislation provides a partial no-fault-based system.

The Welfare State legislation created the Department of Social Security. Victims of accidents at work are now able to claim compensation from the state, without the need to prove negligence. Social security benefits are also available to those who suffer illness or disability.

Should liability in criminal law depend on proof of fault?

Tip

Candidates may be required to consider whether liability should depend on proof of fault. It is important to consider why liability should depend on proof of fault, and the problems that the principle of no liability with proof of fault presents.

Arguments in favour of the requirement of fault in criminal law

The effect of criminal sanctions and procedures

Criminal law is enforced through state procedures and sanctions, focused on the defendant. A guilty verdict will result in the imposition of a sentence on the defendant. The court has a wide range of sentences at its disposal, some of which will directly limit the liberty of the convict, such as electronic tagging, probation and incarceration.

Punishment, however, is only justified if people are at fault. Depriving people of their liberty or imposing other punishments are serious infringements of personal freedom. Furthermore, the liberty of the convicted individual will also be affected by his or her criminal record, which may, for example, prevent access to certain jobs and thus adversely affect opportunities. Opportunities in turn will be affected by the public condemnation of the individual's offence(s). Minor road traffic offences, which are strict liability, do not result in a criminal record, but there is still a stigma attached to strict liability offences, e.g. the butcher who unknowingly sells bad meat.

It is because of these issues that the legal profession, the judges and the legislature regard the principle of no liability without proof of fault as being so important in criminal law.

Strict liability is ineffective

Despite proof of fault being regarded as so important in criminal law, there are some strict liability offences. However, those who argue against strict liability suggest that there is no real evidence that it increases levels of care. This may be partly attributable to the lack of incentive to act reasonably if no account is taken of attempts to prevent the prohibited act occurring. People are also more likely to accept their guilt and punishment if fault has to be proved. In Australia, a defence of all due care is available. Were this defence available in England, it would deal with situations where defendants, such as Mr Shah (in *Harrow LBC* v *Shah*), take all reasonable care to avoid committing the offence.

Furthermore, the argument that in strict liability offences the penalty is small is dubious. It is inconsistent with justice to convict someone who is not guilty in the normal sense of the word just because the penalty is small.

The need to restrain the power of the state

An important argument in favour of the fault requirement is that decisions on guilt rest with juries or independent magistrates, and anything that reduces their capacity to make decisions inevitably means that more power rests with the prosecutors. With most strict liability offences, conviction is a formality.

Arguments in favour of the no-fault principle

Protection of the public

Strict liability legislation is usually justified on the basis that it protects the public good, and typically deals with issues such as public health and safety, protection of the environment and road traffic. Another argument is that higher standards of care are encouraged. Social scientist Barbara Wootten has defended strict liability, suggesting that if the objective of the criminal law is to prevent socially damaging activities, it would be absurd to turn a blind eye to those who cause harm because of carelessness, negligence or even by accident. There is also the fact that strict liability offences carry relatively low sentences in recognition of the lower levels of fault.

Saving of time and expense

There is a further advantage in that court time is saved and consequently costs are reduced when there is no need to prove *mens rea*. Defendants are also more likely to plead guilty. In *Gammon (Hong Kong) Ltd* v *Attorney General of Hong Kong* (1985), the Privy Council said that if the prosecution had to prove *mens rea* in even the smallest regulatory offence, the administration of justice might quickly come to a complete standstill.

Should liability in civil law depend on proof of fault?

In civil law, compensation is regarded as the responsibility of those at fault

Civil law, like criminal law, is based on the notion of individual responsibility. Individuals choose to behave the way they do and should therefore accept responsibility for the outcomes of their actions. Individuals can choose to be more careful so as to minimise the harm they cause. It is not right that individuals who have made the choice to exercise more care should pay for the harm caused by those who have not. However, it is unfair to punish an individual for harm caused by accident, because being more careful would not have prevented the harm and it was not possible for the blameless individual to be more careful.

Gradual move towards a no-fault-based system for accident victims

The advantage of the no-fault-based system for accident victims is that those who are entitled to compensation or social security are more likely to receive it than they would be under the fault-based tort system. It may be fairer for more people to receive compensation, albeit lesser in amount. However, there is the perception of unfairness in that all of society has to pay for what often amounts to the acts of blameworthy individuals.

The Consumer Protection Act 1987

The **Consumer Protection Act 1987** imposes strict liability on producers for damage caused by defective products. This favours the victims, who can recover compensation without the need to prove fault. However, while it is the producer who directly provides the compensation to the claimant, the burden is indirectly borne by society, because as the risk of liability increases, so too will insurance premiums, and this cost will be passed on to consumers.

Insurance premiums

While some victims are able to claim compensation without the need to prove fault, there are many who are still required to do so. Road accident victims and victims of medical errors have to satisfy the negligence requirements, despite the defendants being insured. The insurance issue arguably prevents the extension of no-fault liability as insurance premiums would inevitably have to rise and might become unaffordable. More people would risk driving without insurance and medical practitioners would be less willing to provide anything other than treatment that they considered totally safe.

Conclusion

It would seem that the imposition of liability without fault is more acceptable in civil law than in criminal law. The unfairness of leaving an injured victim without compensation increasingly outweighs the unfairness of blameless individuals being required to provide that compensation indirectly through state funds or insurance.

Despite the arguments against the imposition of strict liability in tort, including the doubt that it raises safety standards, there are areas in which there is no need to prove fault, such as nuisance, *Rylands* v *Fletcher* (1868) and under the principle of vicarious liability.

In criminal law, however, the desire to protect the blameless individual from the outcomes of state procedures and sanctions makes imposition of liability without fault less acceptable. Strict liability offences can only be created by the legislature in limited circumstances.

> **Tip**
>
> Most exam questions require candidates to consider the *extent* to which liability in English law depends upon proof of fault, or *how far* liability in English law depends upon proof of fault. This can be done by explaining and illustrating with material drawn from the specification the general principle of English law that liability does depend upon proof of fault, and then taking the same approach with the exceptions to the general principle. Better candidates will draw on material from a wide range of laws within the criminal and civil law. While many candidates are able to give a broad account of the role of fault in criminal law, relatively few candidates venture far beyond negligence when considering the civil law. Stronger candidates are able to use a wider range of torts, including occupiers' liability, nuisance, *Rylands* v *Fletcher* and the principle of vicarious liability.

Balancing conflicting interests
Theorists

There are several important theorists who ought to be considered in the issue of balancing conflicting interests and whether the law is effective in achieving this.

Karl Marx

Karl Marx (1818–83) believed that law was part of the 'repressive state apparatus' used to ensure the continuing exploitation of the working class (proletariat) by the capitalists (bourgeoisie), i.e. those who own the capital and means of production. For Marx, the law subordinated the interests of the proletariat to those of the bourgeoisie and so did not truly balance conflicting interests. Marx adhered to the conflict model of society and thus was of the view that law did not reconcile conflicting interests in a compromise but rather imposed the interest of one at the expense of another.

Rudolf von Jhering

Rudolf von Jhering (1818–92) believed that the law was a prime method of ordering society. Von Jhering was a utilitarian and more concerned with social than individual aims. His thinking followed that of Jeremy Bentham, whose principle of utility was aimed at maximising human happiness by increasing pleasure and diminishing pain according to the principle of 'the greatest happiness of the greatest number'. He saw society as made up of several competing interests, not all of which could be satisfied. He believed that the interests of the individual would conflict with the interests of society as a whole. The role of the law was to balance interests by reconciling the interests of the individual to society so that they conformed. This was achieved through state-organised coercion, i.e. the law, rewards, duty and love.

Roscoe Pound

Roscoe Pound (1870–1964) divided interests into two main categories: individual interests and social interests. He argued that interests could only be properly balanced if placed on the same plane or level. Thus social interests can be weighed against social interests and individual interests against individual interests. Failure to do this results in a built-in bias in favour of the social interest. Pound thus developed the ideas of von Jhering. He saw law as being developed according to social needs and only serving those interests that lead to the good of society. He subscribed to the consensus model of society, believing that interests should be balanced in accordance with society's values or 'jural postulates'.

The courts have not generally adopted Pound's approach and many of the examples in this guide show the law attempting to balance what are perceived as valuable social interests against the rights of individuals. For example, in *Miller* v *Jackson* (1977), involving an application for an injunction against a cricket club by residents whose properties adjoined the cricket ground, Lord Denning approached the problem in terms of 'a conflict between the interest of the public at large and the interests of a private individual'. Denning concluded that the public interest outweighed the individual one and refused to grant the injunction, although he did attempt to balance this by awarding damages to compensate for the inconvenience of having cricket balls regularly hit into your garden.

To have followed Pound would have necessitated seeing both interests in the same terms, either as individual interests (one person's desire to play cricket against another person's desire to sit in his/her garden) or as social interests (the value to society of protecting domestic privacy against the value of encouraging recreational activities).

Balancing of conflicting interests by Parliament

Legislative process

The balancing of competing interests is to some extent achieved by the process of making an Act of Parliament. The Green Paper invites consultation from various interested parties who may be affected by the proposed legislation. The bill stage of making the legislation requires many debates and votes. There are several political parties reflecting a wide range of views. Before the bill becomes an Act, many compromises and amendments will be made, which take into account the different views of those who are both interested and involved in the legislative process.

It is, however, questionable as to whether a true balance of conflicting interests is actually achieved by the legislative process. There are many powerful interest groups and classes within society. These groups influence the view of ministers, members of Parliament and civil servants. Many politicians are wealthy and influential. They may possess large shareholdings in companies and have directorships or other connections. They may be persuaded more often than they should by groups who are in favour of protecting such interests, despite requirements that these interests should be revealed.

Protective legislation

Parliament sometimes seeks to balance competing interests through legislation, which is advantageous to weaker interest groups. Examples of such protective legislation can be seen in consumer law. The **Consumer Protection Act 1987** imposes strict liability on producers in respect of damage caused by dangerous products. The **Sale and Supply of Goods Act 1994** applies conditions to consumer contracts in respect of title, description, quality and sale by sample. By virtue of the **Unfair Contract Terms Act 1977**, the use of exclusion and limitation clauses by businesses in consumer contracts is significantly reduced.

However, it is questionable how successful such protective legislation is. Phil Harris, in *An Introduction to Law*, points out that such legislation is not rigorously enforced by the state. This, he argues, results in the protective legislation aiding the stronger group while appearing to aid the weaker one. The perceived protection offered to consumers enables businesses to enjoy a better public image and so further their own interests.

A further problem with consumer legislation is that it depends on enforcement by the consumer. Harris believes that most consumers are ignorant of their legislative rights. For example, a shop may tell a customer who has purchased a faulty product that his or her only hope is to deal with the manufacturer direct, or that he or she is only entitled to a credit note, when this is not the case. He also questions whether the average customer would know that a clause in an agreement excluding liability for implied terms is invalid under the **Unfair Contract Terms Act 1977**.

Balancing of conflicting interests by the courts

Judges are more obviously faced with balancing competing interests in the courts, especially in areas such as nuisance, occupiers' liability, crime and consumer law:

- In nuisance, the claimant's interest in being able to enjoy his or her property must be balanced against the interest of his or her neighbours to do what they like with their property.
- In occupiers' liability, the interests of the occupier of land have to be balanced against the interests of people who come onto his or her land.
- In criminal law, the interests of the offender have to be balanced against the interests of society.
- In consumer law, the interests of the consumer have to be balanced against the interests of the business.

Public interests usually outweigh private interests

Pound's theory was that genuine balancing of conflicting interests could only be achieved when the interests were placed in the same category. It is apparent that if the interests in *Miller* v *Jackson* (1977) had been placed in the same category, the outcome may have been different. The interests could have both been placed in the individual category, i.e. Mr Miller's interests in privacy against Mr Jackson's personal interest in playing cricket, or they could have both been placed in the social category, i.e. the public interest in domestic privacy against the public interest in playing cricket.

Protection of national security is another social interest which nearly always prevails if balanced against an individual interest. In *Council of Civil Service Unions* v *Minister for the Civil Service* (1985), the GCHQ case, the prime minister issued an order under which workers at the intelligence-gathering centre were no longer permitted to belong to a trade union. The House of Lords backed the prime minister's order as it was made in the interest of national security, despite the valid argument of the unions that they had not been consulted. When Tony Blair became prime minister, he restored the right of workers to belong to a trade union, making the original threat to national security appear doubtful.

The public interest also outweighs the private interest in respect of most positive rights provided by the European Convention on Human Rights and the **Human Rights Act 1998**. Most of these rights are subject to derogation clauses, which are sometimes drafted in broad terms. In *R (Begum)* v *Headteacher and Governors of Denbigh High School* (2006), Shabina Begum's claim that her right to practise her religion under Article 9 had been violated because the school's uniform policy prevented her wearing the jilbab was unsuccessful. The right to practise a religious belief is subject to limitations that are 'necessary in a democratic society for the protection of the rights and freedoms of others'. The interests of schools in devising uniform policies that are safe, inclusive and uncompetitive outweighs the interest of an individual in being able to wear what he or she wants.

Private interests do sometimes outweigh public interests

Under Article 8 of the European Convention on Human Rights, everyone has the right to respect for his or her private and family life, home and correspondence. However, Article 8 also expressly provides that this right can be overridden 'in the interests of national security, public safety or the economic well-being of the country, for the prevention of disorder or crime, for the protection of health or morals, or for the protection of the rights and freedoms of others'. Thus it seems the rights of individuals will not prevail in the event of a conflict with the public interest. However in *Mosley* v *News Group Newspapers Ltd* (2008), the private interest of the claimant did prevail. This decision provoked an angry response from the editor of the *Daily Mail*, who viewed the decision as an attack on freedom of expression. The private interest under Article 8 also prevailed in *Dickson* v *UK* (2007). The private interest of a prisoner serving life for murder to be able to artificially inseminate a woman he had married since starting his prison sentence prevailed over the public interest in maintaining confidence in the prison system.

A and others v *Secretary of State for the Home Department* (2004) provides another example of the courts deciding in favour of the private interest. The House of Lords decided that the use of s.21 of the **Anti-Terrorism, Crime and Security Act 2001** to detain foreign nationals without charging them was unlawful and an infringement of their human rights. Despite the public interest arguments put forward by the home secretary, the Law Lords were willing to recognise the importance of preserving private interests.

While even the right to life is subject to qualification, some rights, including the right not to be subjected to torture or to inhuman or degrading treatment or punishment (Article 3), are non-derogable and thus ensure that an individual interest cannot be outweighed by a public interest.

Jurors are not part of the permanent state machinery of enforcement. Perhaps, as a result, they are more willing than judges to question claims made by the executive or legislature of threats to national security. In *R* v *Ponting* (1985), a civil servant was charged under the **Official Secrets Act 1911** for leaking information about the sinking of the *Belgrano*, an Argentinian ship, during the Falklands War. Ponting argued that leaking the information was in the public interest because it showed that the British government had not been telling the truth. The judge said that Ponting's argument was no defence. The jury took a different view and acquitted him.

The civil courts and access to justice

Interests can only be balanced if there are institutions available to which aggrieved parties have access on an equal basis. The operation of the rule of law, state-assisted funding of legal actions and the independence of the judiciary ensure that, in theory at least, the court and tribunal system is able to achieve balance.

However, the findings of the Woolf commission (cost, delay and complexity) provide ample evidence that the civil courts often operate in ways which favour powerful organisations and disadvantage individual claimants. It could be argued that tribunals provide a fairer balance in that they have fewer formal procedures and encourage claimants to represent themselves. However, no government funding is available and the ordinary claimant is likely to be facing an opponent who is represented, e.g. an employer or a government department, and this puts him or her at a significant disadvantage. The small claims procedure is also designed to achieve greater balance between the parties and, as with the tribunal system, the emphasis is on informality. But again, there is evidence that the balance remains in favour of the parties who can afford to use lawyers. The majority of cases are brought by businesses trying to recover bad debts rather than by individual claimants.

Balancing conflicting interests in criminal law

Criminal law is concerned with balancing the interests of the offender with those of society. This can be evidenced both in criminal procedure and in the substantive criminal law.

Criminal procedure

The interest of society is the conviction of the guilty and the acquittal of the innocent. The interest of the defendant is to have an assumption of innocence, to be treated with dignity and to have a fair trial. There is also the interest of the victim to consider. The traditional balance of the law in favour of the defendant may leave victims feeling that their interests are not being effectively represented in the criminal process.

There are many aspects that could be considered here and much specific detail can be drawn from Unit 1. Of particular importance are the **Criminal Procedure and Investigation Act 1996**, which allows for the retrial of someone acquitted by a jury where there is evidence of intimidation of witnesses, and the **Criminal Justice Act 2003**, which gives the Court of Appeal the power to order a retrial where 'new and compelling evidence' comes to light after someone has been found not guilty.

In addition, there is the whole issue that surrounds the rights of defendants — burden of proof, rules on arrest, rules of evidence, right to silence, effect of not-guilty finding —

and how these rules are designed to create balance between the prosecution and the defence. It is important to address the question of whether the balance has now swung too far in favour of the prosecution, and to look at the right to silence and the effect of s.34 of the **Criminal Justice and Public Order Act 1994,** which allow juries or magistrates to draw inferences from a defendant failing to mention, when under caution, facts later relied on in his defence. Another example is the issue of whether an accused person should be entitled to bail. The **Bail Act 1976** created a presumption in favour of bail. The courts are obliged to grant bail unless one of the exceptions applies. This Act seeks to ensure the liberty of the accused until the trial. The court has to balance the interest of the public in being protected and the interest of the individual in being presumed innocent until proven guilty. There has been a shift towards the public interest in recent years, with legislation increasingly providing circumstances in which bail may or must be refused.

In each of these areas of criminal law, recent developments have therefore involved restricting the rights of defendants and placing greater emphasis on the interests of society and the victims of crime.

Substantive criminal law: the defence of intoxication

The public interest lies in being protected from those who cause harm when drunk. The individual interest lies in being held less responsible for actions carried out while intoxicated (and thus with limited *mens rea*) than for actions carried out with full awareness.

The availability of the defence of intoxication varies according to circumstances. Where the accused is involuntarily intoxicated, intoxication can be a defence to any crime, provided the accused lacks the necessary *mens rea*. Voluntary intoxication, however, can only be a defence to a crime of specific intent. The courts regard voluntary intoxication as reckless in itself and recklessness is the level of *mens rea* required for crimes of basic intent. In *DPP* v *Majewski* (1977), the House of Lords refused to allow voluntary intoxication to be used as a defence to a basic intent offence. Lord Steyn said that one of the prime purposes of the criminal law is the protection from unprovoked violence of people who are pursuing their lawful lives; to allow intoxication as a defence would be to leave the citizen unprotected from such violence. The House of Lords was of the opinion that to allow voluntary intoxication as a defence would not provide a proper balance between the interests of the defendant and the interests of society as a whole.

The concept of strict liability

In the creation of strict liability crimes, the law may suppress the interests of the individual in the interest of public safety. The **Rivers (Prevention of Pollution) Act 1951** makes it a criminal offence to pollute rivers, without the need to prove such pollution is caused intentionally, recklessly or negligently. In *Alphacell* v *Woodward* (1972) the defendants were found guilty of polluting a river, despite the fact that they were not negligent and were unaware of the mechanical breakdown of their equipment, which usually prevented such pollution occurring. One justification for strict liability in situations like this is that it works to the disadvantage of the more powerful interest and thus helps to achieve balance.

Balancing conflicting interests in the law of tort

The law of tort is mainly concerned with balancing two individual interests. However, public interests sometimes arise, as seen earlier when considering *Miller* v *Jackson* (1977). In that case, the public interest was considered when determining whether to award an injunction.

Negligence

The interest of one individual in not being harmed through another's carelessness has to be balanced against the interest of the other individual in not being held liable for unforeseeable and remote consequences.

In the law on psychiatric injury, the law limits liability to secondary victims by applying stringent criteria not applied to primary victims. Primary victims, e.g. those directly involved in an accident, can clearly be foreseen as being likely to be affected by the defendant's actions. However, the courts apply restrictions on who can claim as a result of seeing or hearing something happen to someone else. It was made clear in *Alcock* v *Chief Constable of South Yorkshire* (1991) and *Page* v *Smith* (1995) that a secondary victim must prove five additional criteria:

(1) he or she is a person of ordinary phlegm
(2) he or she has close ties of love and affection with those in the accident
(3) he or she is close in time and space
(4) he or she perceived the accident with his or her own unaided senses
(5) it can be shown that psychiatric illness rather than just physical injury was foreseeable

Whether a true balancing of conflicting interests is achieved by these criteria is questionable. The trauma of a person identifying a body in a mortuary or seeing an accident on television could be just as great as a qualifying claimant, but the court has to consider the interests of the defendant as well. It is arguably not fair to allow claims from people not directly involved in the accident, unless they are foreseeable claimants.

Nuisance

The law of private nuisance is concerned with balancing the competing interests of neighbours to enjoy their property. Any interference which is unreasonable is unlawful. In deciding whether the level of interference is unreasonable, the courts take into account factors such as locality, sensitivity and malice. For example in *Laws* v *Florinplace Ltd* (1981), when a shop in a residential area was converted into a sex shop and cinema club, locality was a relevant factor, and in *Hollywood Silver Fox Farm* v *Emmett*

(1936), the claim succeeded because the defendant had deliberately set out to cause harm.

Tip

For the examination, candidates are expected to explore a variety of ways in which the law seeks to achieve a balancing of conflicting interests. Better candidates will consider both the law made by the legislature and the decisions made by the courts, and also the processes by which such laws are made. The interests which are being balanced should be clearly identified — a frequent omission of weaker candidates. Examples to illustrate the balancing of conflicting interests can be taken from virtually any part of the law specification. What is important is to make sure that the examples are used appropriately. You need to keep referring to the interests that are in conflict, the ways in which the law is attempting to balance them and the extent to which a successful balancing of conflicting interests is achieved.

Conclusion

It is clear that there is an attempt to balance conflicting interests both in the creation of legislation and in the courts.

The consultation process and bill stage of making legislation ensure that a range of interests is at least considered, but it is questionable whether a true balancing of conflicting interests is achieved due to the influence of powerful and wealthy interest groups. In civil law, an attempt is made to strengthen the weaker party through protective legislation. However, the effectiveness of this legislation is reliant on individuals having the knowledge, tenacity, financial means and time to enforce their rights. In criminal law, legislative developments concerning criminal procedure appear to place greater importance on the interests of society and the victims of crime.

In the courts, judges can be seen to attempt a balancing of conflicting interests both in the decision and the remedy/sanction. While there are some exceptions, judges arguably continue to favour the public interest over the private interest. For example, the law relating to psychiatric injury has clearly been developed based on policy — to limit the number of claims being brought before the courts and to keep insurance premiums to affordable levels. The same can be said regarding the refusal of the House of Lords to allow voluntary intoxication as a defence to crimes of basic intent.

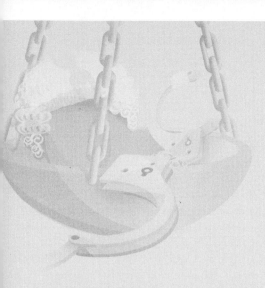

Questions
&
Answers

This section provides you with five questions, which cover all the Unit 4 Concepts of Law areas. In this examination paper, all the questions are set as essays and they are not subdivided.

There will be a choice of three questions, of which you must answer one. Candidates are required to write a continuous piece of prose. However, the questions do usually ask candidates to consider more than one aspect, and the A-grade answers provided in this section should give you a clear idea of the approach and structure required.

Remember that despite the allocation of 30 marks to this question, you are, as stated in the AQA specification, expected to write 'an hour-long essay'.

Examples and supporting evidence for questions in Unit 4 Concepts of Law can be taken from anywhere across the whole AS and A2 specifications. You will notice that some of the candidate answers in this section follow the material used in this guide quite closely. However, it would be possible to write A-grade answers to each of the questions using entirely different material. What matters in Unit 4 Concepts of Law answers is how the material is used and how it relates to the ideas in the question.

Each question is followed by an A-grade answer. These are strong responses and students may be able to attain a Grade A with less material than these answers contain.

To acquire the necessary skills and become more familiar with this style of examination question, it is a good idea to practise adapting the A-grade answers for different questions. You are strongly encouraged to download past papers and mark schemes from AQA (**www.aqa.org.uk**) or to obtain these from your teacher.

Examiner's comments

The candidate answers are accompanied by examiner's comments, preceded by the icon ℮. These help explain the elements of the answer for which marks can be awarded and are intended to give you an insight into what examiners are looking for.

Law and morality

Write a critical analysis of the relationship between law and morals (30 marks)

■ ■ ■

A-grade answer

There have been many different views expressed by theorists regarding the relationship between law and morals, and these views have influenced many legal reforms. It is useful to begin with an explanation of the characteristics of, and distinctions between, legal and moral rules, before proceeding to explore areas of coincidence and areas of divergence.

Law was described by Sir John Salmond as 'the body of principles recognised and applied by the state in the administration of justice'. Breach of legal rules will result in state sanctions and procedures. In criminal law there are sanctions such as imprisonment. In civil law the wrongdoer is usually ordered to compensate the victim. Other characteristics of legal rules are that they take effect at a precise time and require compulsory compliance by all members of society. An example is the ban on smoking in public places, which has applied to everyone since the Smoke-free (Premises and Enforcement) Regulations came into effect on 1 July 2007.

Society's code of morality is defined by Phil Harris as a set of beliefs, values, principles and standards of behaviour. Unlike legal rules, compliance with moral rules is voluntary and enforcement is informal, usually through social or domestic pressure. Moral rules develop usually over long periods of time, as conduct becomes increasingly acceptable or unacceptable. In a pluralistic society, however, such as that in the UK, the moral duties of individuals vary. For example, while some individuals regard abortion, homosexuality, euthanasia and arranged marriages as immoral, others do not.

The relationship between legal and moral rules can be described as two intersecting circles. The intersection represents the coincidence of law and morals, and the areas outside the intersection represent areas of divergence.

Long-established rules, for example those prohibiting murder or theft, can be traced back to a moral source, this being the Ten Commandments. However, there are many ways in which legal and moral rules may come to coincide.

Judicial reform of the law may be influenced by public morality. In the criminal law, the House of Lords decision in *R* v *R* (1991) was influenced by the moral rule that a husband should not force his wife to have sexual intercourse. In tort, the decision in *Chadwick* v *British Railways Board* (1967) concerning the duty owed to rescuers who suffer psychiatric injury was influenced by the moral rule that people ought to help others who may be in trouble.

Legislative reform may also be influenced by public morality. For example, as public morality has shifted toward a greater acceptance of homosexuality, the legislature has responded. The Sexual Offences Act 1967 legalised homosexuality between consenting males over the age of 21. In 1994 the age was reduced to 18 and in December 2000 it was reduced to 16. In December 2005, the Civil Partnership Act 2004 came into effect, allowing civil registrations that give gay and lesbian couples some of the same legal entitlements as married couples.

In turn, it can be argued that legislation is sometimes introduced with the aim of educating the public to consider certain behaviour morally wrong. An example is the discrimination legislation, which aims to educate the public not to discriminate on the basis of sex, age or disability.

While there is a considerable overlap of legal and moral rules, the pluralistic nature of society means that the coincidence is partial. Britain has a population of mixed cultures and races, of mixed political ideals and of differing religious followings. It can perhaps be argued that there is no public consensus on any moral issue. Cases in which the judiciary has had to consider differing moral positions include *Gillick* v *West Norfolk and Wisbech Area Health Authority* (1986), *Re A (Children)* (2000), *ex parte Diane Pretty* (2001) and the Debbie Purdy case (2009). Parliament also has to take into account the differing views of the population, and within Parliament itself many different views are held. This was illustrated at the second reading of the Human Fertilization and Embryology Bill in May 2008, when MPs voted against reducing the 24-week abortion limit to 20 weeks by 332 votes to 190.

Statements reflecting the pluralistic nature of society can be found in the Hart–Devlin debate. The Sexual Offences Act 1967 was introduced following recommendations made by the Wolfenden Committee in its 1957 report. The report prompted the debate. Professor Hart drew on the work of Professor John Stuart Mill who, in his essay 'On liberty', stated: '...the only part of the conduct of anyone, for which he is amenable to society, is that which concerns others...Over himself, over his own body and mind, the individual is sovereign'. Hart and Mill believed it was immoral to make the minority conform to the will of the majority when in private. They recognised the pluralistic nature of society and the importance of individual liberty. Lord Devlin's views are more reflective of the late nineteenth-century criminal judge Sir James Stephen. Devlin believed that the loosening of moral bonds would lead to the disintegration of society. The law should punish acts which offend the common morality, whether done in public or in private.

Sir John Wolfenden followed the views of Mill and Hart. Their views were reflected in other reforming legislation of that decade including the Obscene Publications Act 1968 and the Divorce Law Reform Act 1969. The majority of the House of Lords in *Gillick* v *West Norfolk and Wisbech Area Health Authority* (1986) also adopted the Mill and Hart approach.

However, the influence of Stephen and Devlin can be seen in a number of judicial decisions. Perhaps the most significant recent decision is that of the House of Lords in *R* v *Brown* (1993) and the European Court of Human Rights in *Laskey, Brown and Jaggard* v *United Kingdom* (1997). The House of Lords held that the defence of consent could not be used in respect of sadomasochistic acts, which in this case were conducted in private. The European Court of Human Rights upheld the decision. Infringement of Article 8, the right to respect for private life, was justified by the need to protect health or morals.

Interpretation of Article 8 is also at the heart of the assisted suicide cases. The European Court of Human Rights and the national courts continue to show preference for Devlin's view. In these cases, the claimants argue that the law preventing people from deciding when to end their own lives breaches the right to respect for private and family life.

The broad overlap of legal and moral rules is perhaps due to the characteristics they share. Both are concerned to impose certain standards of conduct without which it is difficult for society to exist, and both employ normative language. Laws, as Harris states, 'are found side by side with moral codes of greater or less complexity'.

There are, however, areas of divergence. There appears to be little moral justification for tobacco and alcohol consumption being legal and smoking of cannabis illegal. There are also moral rules which are not reinforced by legal rules. An example is the moral duty to help people who are in danger. The general position (there are exceptions) is that there is no legal liability for failing to act.

Natural law theorists would argue that legal rules which have no moral connection should not be afforded the status of law. According to Lloyd, the common thread running through the different views expressed as to what natural law is, is 'the constant assertion that there are objective moral principles which depend upon the nature of the universe'. Aristotle believed that the laws of nature constituted the natural law. St Thomas Aquinas believed that natural law was the divine law. In the mid-twentieth century, Professor Lon Fuller referred to the inner morality of law. To be valid, the law had to conform to certain procedural requirements including consistency and being prospective.

In contrast, the positivists believe that whether a law is good or bad it is still valid. The origins of John Austin's command theory, whereby law is a command from a sovereign and enforced by a sanction, can be traced to Jeremy Bentham and Hobbes. Jeremy Bentham rejected natural law theories as 'nonsense on stilts'. Natural law was based on unprovable principles. What the law is, and what the law ought to be, should be treated as different issues.

Professor Hart also subscribes to the positivist view. From 1958 to 1967, a debate took place between Hart and Fuller. This was sparked by the views of the German philosopher Gustav Radbruch. According to Radbruch and Fuller, the Nazi laws which permitted atrocities should not have been regarded as valid. This was the view later adopted by the German courts. Hart, however, considered that the laws were legally valid but should have been challenged by people prepared to take the legal consequences.

In conclusion, it can be seen that there is a close relationship between legal and moral rules. A substantial body of English law is based on moral rules. The extent to which law should be influenced by morality remains topical. While it can be argued that a significant section of society has come to adopt the view taken by Professor Hart, there nevertheless remains a widely shared belief that weakening of the moral basis of law is dangerous.

This is a well-structured, comprehensive and yet concisely written answer. Good use is made of material drawn from many areas of the specification. Theories of the relationship between law and morality are soundly explained and illustrative material is used to demonstrate the influence of the theories on the development of the law.

This is a very good answer that would gain 29 or 30 marks.

Law and justice

Discuss the meaning of law and justice and consider the relationship between them. (30 marks)

■ ■ ■

A-grade answer

The law is a set of standardised procedures and mechanisms used in the enforcement of basic rights and the regulation of society. Sir John Salmond defined law as 'the principles used in the administration of justice'. In *The Concept of Law*, H. L. A. Hart classified law in terms of primary rules that impose certain duties and rules of adjudication, which provide for authoritative decisions to be made when disputes arise. Legal rules are thus characterised by having a specific point of creation, by requiring compulsory compliance, and by the consequences of state sanctions and procedures should they be breached.

Justice is more difficult to define than law. Basically, it can be viewed as 'the principle of fairness', but this then leads to a discussion as to what 'fairness' means. This has led to many differing definitions of justice being put forward. Justice, according to the law, can be formal, substantive, distributive or corrective, or any combination of these types.

Formal justice, often referred to as procedural justice, requires equality of treatment in accordance with the classification laid down by rules. Formal justice therefore requires adherence to the rules of natural justice and the rule of law. Natural justice is based on two principles: each party should have the opportunity to be heard; and no one should be judge in his or her own cause. Judicial independence is fundamental to natural justice and can be seen operating in *R v Bow Street Metropolitan Stipendiary Magistrates, ex parte Pinochet* (1999), in which the House of Lords decided that the former dictator of Chile should be extradited to Spain to face serious charges of human rights abuse. When it was revealed that Lord Hoffman, one of the Law Lords who heard the case, had links with Amnesty International, a human rights organisation involved in the proceedings, the House of Lords annulled the decision and reheard the case without Lord Hoffman. Similarly, in *Morrison v AWG Group Ltd and another* (2006) the Court of Appeal held that a High Court judge should have stood down from hearing the case. He had acknowledged that he had known a witness for some 30 years, and consequently that witness was replaced. The judge then heard the case. Lord Justice Mummery stated that in such situations judges should stand down to avoid any perception of bias, however unjustified such a perception might be.

The theory of the rule of law, as outlined by Dicey in *An Introduction to the Study of the Law of the Constitutions* (1885), is that 'no person is punishable except for a distinct breach of the law established in the courts' and also that no man is 'above the law, but that every man, whatever his rank, is subject to the ordinary law of the realm'.

question

One way in which the rule of law is guaranteed is by having an independent judiciary able to review the decisions of politicians and public officials. The process of judicial review examines whether the body or individual in question was within their rights in making the decision. If a decision is *ultra vires* ('beyond the powers'), it can be quashed. Procedural *ultra vires* arises where proper procedures have not been followed, e.g. there has been a breach of natural justice as in the Pinochet case. Substantive *ultra vires* arises where the content of the decision was outside the power of the body that made it. In some cases, the reliance by governments on the requirements of national security has arguably inhibited judicial review of their decisions. However, the passing of the Human Rights Act 1998 has enabled judges to review even primary legislation to determine whether it complies with the European Convention on Human Rights. In *A and others* v *Secretary of State for the Home Department* (2004), the House of Lords decided that the detention of foreign nationals without trial under s.21 of the Anti-terrorism, Crime and Security Act 2001 was not justified, despite the government's argument that they were a threat to national security. The legislative provisions in this case clearly contravened the rule of law because the suspects were being punished before being found by the courts to have broken the law.

Breaches of formal justice deny justice to both defendants and victims. The miscarriage of justice cases in the 1980s and 1990s arising from IRA bombings suggested that the police had compromised some of the principles of formal justice. In particular, there were concerns about confessions, the treatment of defendants while in custody and the reliability of forensic evidence. Upon releasing Judith Ward, the Court of Appeal referred to the failure to disclose evidence in her case and the consequence of denying a fair trial. However, the system did arguably deliver justice, because the convictions were quashed and compensation was paid to those wrongly convicted. Furthermore, the Criminal Appeals Act 1995 now provides for an appeal if the Court of Appeal thinks the conviction is 'unsafe', regardless of technicalities.

Victims are denied justice when the system fails to secure a conviction due to breaches in formal justice. The Macpherson Inquiry, following the Stephen Lawrence murder, concluded that the police investigation was 'marred by a combination of professional incompetence, institutional racism and a failure of leadership by senior officers'. Both the public and private prosecutions failed to secure convictions of the suspects. Influenced partly by the injustice of this particular case, the Criminal Justice Act 2003 was passed to allow for people acquitted of certain serious offences to be retried where there is new and compelling evidence and it is in the interests of justice to have a retrial.

Substantive justice is concerned with whether rules are inherently 'fair'. Attempts to define 'fair' have led to many differing definitions or theories of justice.

Natural law theorists believe that there is a higher order of law and if this is followed, laws are just. If not, then not only is the law not just, but it cannot be considered a law at all and need not be obeyed. St Thomas Aquinas, for example, argued that law is God-given and therefore, if the laws based on Christian teaching are followed, the result will be justice. A law which went against this God-derived law would always be 'unjust' and should not be obeyed.

The Human Rights Act would suggest that there is a close connection between the law and the natural law theorists' concept of justice, because it incorporates into English law the European Convention on Human Rights which sets out 'fundamental' rights, such as freedom of expression and freedom from torture. Natural law theorists would not support the Law Lords' decision in the Debbie Purdy case (2009) because it does not uphold the sanctity of human life.

An alternative theory is that of utilitarianism, argued by Jeremy Bentham, which measures the justice of a law on the basis of its consequences — if it benefits the majority, then it is just. This means that a law may create social inequalities, but if the gain to the majority exceeds the loss to the minority, then it is just. Utilitarian principles arguably underpin English law because Parliament, the sovereign law maker, is elected. The legislative process is democratic and should ensure that legislation is created only if it pleases the majority. However, it can be argued that the population plays a small part in statute creation because MPs vote along party lines and the government only has to answer to the electorate every 5 years in an election.

John Rawls developed the idea of a just society being one that a group of rational but mutually disinterested people, in 'the original position' and behind a 'veil of ignorance', would unanimously choose to belong to if such a choice were available. He rejected the argument of utilitarianism and argued that inequality can only be just if that inequality is of benefit to all, not merely to the greatest number. He also argued that liberty must be respected and cannot be limited to promote greater happiness. The European Convention on Human Rights reflects Rawls's theory of justice in that individuals are given the positive rights he regards as important, including freedom of speech and assembly, freedom from arbitrary arrest and seizure. However the derogation clauses depart from Rawls's theory, allowing for a denial of rights, for example 'in the interests of national security, public safety or the economic well-being of the country, for the prevention of disorder or crime, for the protection of health or morals, or for the protection of the rights and freedoms of others' (Article 8). Only the last point arguably reflects Rawls's theory, in that liberty can be limited if it will result in greater liberty overall.

The Greek philosopher Aristotle introduced the principles of distributive and corrective justice. Distributive justice is concerned with the fair allocation of benefits and burdens within society, while corrective justice requires the righting of wrongs through fair remedy or punishment. Distributive justice is also subscribed to by Rawls and it is clear that the English legal system is based on the idea of distributive justice in that the law does allocate benefits and burdens through rights and duties, and perhaps more obviously through the taxation system. Corrective justice then operates through the system of state sanctions imposed in criminal law and remedies provided to the victim in civil law. Nozick, however, rejected the distributive theory, preferring the entitlement theory in which the state should only intervene to protect natural rights. The state should therefore play a minimal role and redistribution of individuals' rights is not justified for any social purpose. The English legal system goes further than merely enforcing natural rights and does not comply with Nozick's theory of the minimal state.

It is clear that there are aspects of English law where the requirement for formal justice has not been met. This is also true of substantive justice, although arguably less so. However legislative reforms including the Criminal Justice Act and Criminal Appeals Act have helped to ensure that procedures are fairer and individuals are more likely to experience justice. Arguably, substantive justice does underpin the English legal system, and in the miscarriage of justice cases, for example, it was not the substantive law that was in question but the manner in which it was being administered.

It remains true of course that substantive law can be changed through enactment so that laws regarded as unjust can be repealed. It is not so simple to alter the behaviour of those administering the legal system, making formal justice more difficult to achieve.

This is a thoughtful and well-argued answer. There is a concise definition of law, but the meaning of justice is explored fully and a number of theories are identified. The student has avoided the weaker approach of writing a description of the theories followed by a series of examples of justice in practice. Instead, this answer genuinely tries to link ideas about justice with examples drawn from other areas of the specification that illustrate them.

The candidate also recognises that the question is about the connection between law and justice, and this is frequently referred to and brought into the conclusion.

This is a very good answer, which would gain 27 or 28 marks out of 30.

Judicial creativity

Referring to precedent and statutory interpretation, discuss how creative judges can be, and compare their contribution to the development of the law with that of Parliament. (30 marks)

■ ■ ■

A-grade answer

The constitutional role of the judiciary is to apply the law that Parliament makes. However, judges have the power to change rules or make new rules through precedent or statutory interpretation.

The doctrine of precedent is based on the requirement that judges must follow decisions made in earlier cases, and on the face of it would seem to limit their freedom to be creative. First of all, there is the hierarchy of the courts, which means that courts are bound by decisions of other courts higher up in the hierarchy. Under the 1966 Practice Direction, the House of Lords is allowed to depart from its own earlier decisions, as, for example, in *Hetherington* v *British Rail* and *R* v *Shivpuri*, but the Court of Appeal is bound by its own earlier decisions, despite Lord Denning's efforts to free it from these constraints. The binding part of the judgement is called the *ratio decidendi* and later courts are bound to follow the legal principles on which the decision was based if their case contains similar facts.

However, judges are able to exercise considerable creativity, despite the constraints of precedent. In some areas of law, like contract law, negligence and fatal offences, judges make nearly all the legal rules. An example of a very creative judgement was *Donoghue* v *Stevenson*, which established the modern law of negligence. Another good example is *R* v *R*, which introduced the idea that a husband could be guilty of rape if he forced his wife to have sex.

The House of Lords can use the Practice Direction and so, in theory, has almost unlimited power to change earlier precedents. In fact, it uses this power with restraint, but on several occasions it has exercised creativity and brought about significant changes in the law. Examples are that duress cannot be used as a defence to a murder charge (*R* v *Howe*, 1987), that *Hansard* can, in certain circumstances, be referred to when interpreting a statute (*Pepper* v *Hart*, 1993), and that the *mens rea* of recklessness should always be subjective (*R* v *G*, 2003, overruling *R* v *Caldwell*, 1982).

There are also other ways that courts can be creative. Sometimes there is no precedent and judges can use legal reasoning and persuasive precedents. For example, the law on negligent misstatement was developed from the dissenting judgement of Lord Denning in *Candler* v *Crane Christmas* (1951). Areas of law can also be developed from *obiter dicta* statements. The neighbour principle, set out in the House of Lords in

Donoghue v *Stevenson* (1932), is regarded as the foundation of the modern law of negligence. Judges can also distinguish the case from the precedent by arguing that the facts are materially different. *Merritt* v *Merritt* did not follow the earlier case of *Balfour* v *Balfour* because although both cases concerned agreements between husbands and wives, in the latter case they were separated. Higher courts can, of course, reverse decisions of lower courts, as in *Gillick* and *Tomlinson* v *Congleton BC*, where the House of Lords reversed the Court of Appeal decision, and it can overrule earlier precedents by lower courts.

When interpreting statutes, courts have less opportunity to be creative. Their powers are largely limited to explaining ambiguous or unclear wording, though sometimes they are asked to rule on wording which is clear but seems to go against common sense or the spirit of the Act. In all these situations they have aids to help them, which allow some creativity. For example, they can refer to other parts of the Act or to a report, e.g. by the Law Commission on which the Act was based. Following the decision in *Pepper* v *Hart*, they can also refer to ministerial statements in Parliament in certain limited circumstances.

What is much more controversial is whether judges should be able to change the wording of a statute to arrive at what it is presumed Parliament intended to say. Supporters of the literal rule, such as Viscount Simmonds, say that to do this would be to usurp the role of Parliament and therefore be wrong. But creative judges like Lord Denning argued that it was the duty of the court to fill in the gaps and look for what Parliament intended to say. When judges use the mischief rule/purposive approach, they are in effect prepared to change the literal and often clear meaning of words in order to arrive at what Parliament intended. For example, in *Royal College of Nursing* v *DHSS*, the Abortion Act case, they changed 'by a registered medical practitioner' to 'under the supervision of…', in order to promote the intention of Parliament in the provision of access to legal safe abortion. The purposive approach allows for a broader interpretation of a word or phrase than the literal rule. In *R* v *Cockburn* (2008), the defendant had been convicted under the Offences Against the Person Act of setting a 'mantrap or other engine…with intent to cause grievous bodily harm'. Upholding the conviction, the Court of Appeal referred to the purpose of the Act. It held that a spiked metal object attached to the roof of a shed in such a way that it would fall on anyone opening the shed door was an engine. The defendant had claimed that the device was operated by gravity and was therefore not an engine.

Judges who follow the literal rule will be less creative. They prefer the security of preserving the status quo and offer as justification their respect of parliamentary sovereignty. *Fisher* v *Bell* is a good example. It was clear under contract law that a knife in a shop window was not being 'offered' for sale, because displays of goods in shop windows are invitations to treat, not offers. Therefore, applying the literal rule, the defendant was not guilty. Parliament had created this situation through its wording in the Act and in the judge's view, it was the role of Parliament to change it.

Judges can use the 'golden rule', where the wording creates an absurd or repugnant situation as in *Sigsworth* (where, if taken literally, the Act would allow a man to inherit from his mother, whom he had murdered) or *Adler* v *George*, in which the defendant could have escaped criminal liability had a literal interpretation of the word 'vicinity' been applied.

It seems that in more recent times judges are being encouraged to use the purposive approach and thus be more creative. This is partly because of the influence of the European Union law, which is drafted in general terms and assumes judges will fill in the detail. Also of great importance is the Human Rights Act, which allows judges to consider whether an Act complies with the European Convention on Human Rights.

When comparing the roles of Parliament and judges, it is obvious that there is a place for both in law making. In many areas of law, Parliament has chosen not to become involved and increasingly it has less time for law reform. There is nothing anti-democratic in judges making new principles of law, as long as Parliament has the right ultimately to overrule the decision.

Parliament is able to be much more creative than judges for several reasons. First, unlike judges, it can choose the time to legislate. Judges have to wait for a suitable case to be brought. In addition, judges can only consider evidence presented by the parties in the case. They cannot consider arguments about the general social, economic or moral aspects, even though their decision, e.g. in *Gillick*, may have implications for society generally. When Parliament legislates, the views of all interested people or groups are actively sought.

Judges can only make law on the facts before them and cannot, unlike Parliament, set out a code of rules to cover all similar situations. It does not help when one small change is made, e.g. the reintroduction of gross negligence manslaughter in *Prentice/Adomako*, when really the whole area needs to be properly reformed. Also, judge-made law operates retrospectively and can thus seem unfair. The decision in *R* v *R* (1991), creating the offence of husband rape, turned an act that was lawful at the time it was committed into a serious criminal offence. However the decision was upheld by the European Court of Human Rights on the basis that judicial law-making was well entrenched in legal tradition and the development of the law on this issue had been foreseeable. This reasoning was also applied by the Court of Appeal — *R* v *Crooks* (2004) — in upholding the conviction of a man who had intercourse with his wife without her consent 32 years before his conviction and 21 years before the decision in *R* v *R*.

Another problem is that changing the law frequently creates uncertainty, and this explains why the House of Lords is reluctant to use the Practice Direction (e.g. in *Knuller* it would not overrule *Shaw*). Certainty is particularly important in certain areas of law such as crime, and many judges prefer to leave reform of the criminal law to Parliament. For example, the judiciary has resisted pressure to reform the law on assisted suicide. In rejecting an appeal by Debbie Purdy, who had wanted the law clarified to enable her husband to assist her suicide without fear of prosecution, Lord Judge in the Court of Appeal in February 2009 said: 'It is no part of the court's function to enter into that debate. The proper forum for that discussion is Parliament.' The decision was then overturned in the House of Lords in July the same year.

In conclusion, it can be seen that judges can be creative, but that they are and should be less creative than Parliament. It is also evident that judges are playing a more significant creative role because of the UK's membership of the European Union and because of the Human Rights Act.

This is a full answer, packed with relevant examples from several parts of the specification.

The question asks you to cover a lot of material. It requires some reference to precedent and statutory interpretation and how the rules affect the ability of judges to be creative. It then requires a comparison with the way Parliament works. This answer deals with all these aspects and is clearly structured and systematic.

One of its strengths is that it never becomes a purely descriptive answer. It frequently refers back to the question and makes appropriate analytical comment.

It is a balanced and clear answer and would be awarded 29 or 30 marks.

Fault

'It is a principle of fundamental importance in English law that there should be no liability without fault.'

Consider how far fault is an essential requirement of liability in English law, and discuss the suggestion that fault should be an essential requirement. (30 marks)

■ ■ ■

A-grade answer

Both the *Concise Oxford Dictionary* and the *Collins Concise Dictionary* define fault in terms of 'responsibility' and 'culpability' or 'blame' for something wrong. Responsibility is defined by both dictionaries in terms of ability to take rational decisions, and rational is defined by both dictionaries in terms of reasonableness. Perhaps the core meaning of fault to emerge through these definitions is 'responsibility for something wrong', although the other definitions will also feature in the ensuing discussion.

Fault is generally an essential requirement of liability in the law of tort. Liability in negligence requires proof of a breach of duty. A breach of duty arises when the defendant fails to act, or not act, as the 'reasonable man' would have done. In *Bolton* v *Stone* (1951), the defendants would have acted as the 'reasonable man' by erecting a high fence around the ground to minimise the risk of people outside the ground being injured by cricket balls. Liability under the Occupiers' Liability Act 1957 also requires proof of fault. Under s.2(2)(b) a lower duty of care is owed to people on the premises in exercise of their calling, than to other visitors. In *Roles* v *Nathan* (1963), the occupiers were not liable when chimney sweeps died from inhaling fumes. They had warned the sweeps of the risk, and it was the responsibility of the sweeps to be aware of the danger. A similar rationale is behind the 1984 Act, which regulates the duty owed to trespassers. Most people would argue that an occupier should be less at fault in respect of injury to trespassers than injury to lawful visitors. The duty owed to trespassers is limited to certain circumstances, which have proved difficult for adult trespassers in particular to establish. The courts are reluctant to impose liability in this area, as illustrated by *Tomlinson* v *Congleton Borough Council* (2003). The claimant, who was 18, dived into a lake in a public park and suffered a severe spinal injury. The council was not liable. It had placed warning signs in the area and was planning to make the lake inaccessible to the public when the accident occurred.

Fault is also relevant to the general defence of contributory negligence. Under the Law Reform (Contributory Negligence) Act 1945 s.1(1), damages are reduced according to the claimant's responsibility for the damage. In *Froom* v *Butcher* (1976), the claimant's damages were reduced by 25% due to his failure to wear a seat belt.

There are, however, areas of tort in which there is no need to prove fault. For example, nuisance is a strict liability tort. The defendant cannot claim as a defence that he/she took reasonable care to avoid causing the nuisance. The rule in *Rylands* v *Fletcher* is another strict liability tort. However, since the case of *Cambridge Water Co. Ltd* v *Eastern Counties Leather* (1994), negligence principles have applied in respect of the type of damage caused having to be foreseeable.

It is important also to consider the principle of vicarious liability, which imposes liability for someone else's fault. In the workplace, the employer is liable for torts committed by employees during the course of their employment. This includes torts committed while the employee is doing what he/she is authorised to do but doing it in an unauthorised manner. In *Rose* v *Plenty* (1976), the employer had expressly forbidden employees to allow people to ride on the milk floats. The employer was, nevertheless, vicariously liable, when a 13-year-old boy was injured while helping an employee deliver milk.

So far, we have considered how fault is generally a requirement for liability in tort, albeit that there are some exceptions. There is also a general principle of no liability without proof of fault in criminal law.

To be found guilty of most criminal offences an *actus reus* and *mens rea* must be present. The *actus reus* must usually be committed voluntarily. If the accused is not in control of his/her actions, the defendant cannot be considered to be at fault and there are general defences that the accused may raise, including insanity, automatism and duress. In *R* v *Bailey* (1983), the accused, a diabetic, successfully pleaded the defence of automatism.

The *mens rea* comprises the mental element of the crime. All of the non-fatal offences except that provided by s.18 of the Offences Against the Person Act 1861 are crimes of basic intent. Section 18 is a specific intent crime. All the non-fatal offences, therefore, require proof of fault for a conviction. Similarly, all homicide offences require proof of fault. Murder is the most serious homicide offence. The accused must intend to kill or cause grievous bodily harm. The seriousness of the offence is recognised in the mandatory sentence of life imprisonment.

While fault is a requirement for liability in most crimes, there are examples of offences for which the *actus reus* is more serious than the *mens rea*. This can be seen in the law relating to non-fatal and fatal offences. Section 47 of the Offences Against the Person Act 1861 (OAPA) requires actual bodily harm to be caused to the victim, but the defendant only needs intention or recklessness to cause an assault or battery. Section 20 of the OAPA requires grievous bodily harm or wounding to be caused to the victim, but the defendant only needs intention or recklessness to cause some harm. In constructive manslaughter, the *mens rea* is only that required for the act which causes the death, and in murder cases a defendant can be convicted on the basis of having the intention to cause grievous bodily harm. Clearly, a defendant convicted of these crimes does not have the level of fault to match the consequence.

The fault requirement dwindles further in strict liability and absolute liability offences. Strict liability crimes have no fault requirement in terms of *mens rea*. There is, however, a fault requirement in that the *actus reus* must be committed voluntarily. In *Smedleys* v *Breed* (1974), the defendants were convicted despite having taken all reasonable precautions to prevent contamination of their food products occurring. Absolute liability crimes, however, have no fault requirement either in respect of *mens rea* or the *actus reus*. In *Winzar* v *Chief Constable of Kent* (1983), the accused was convicted of being found drunk on the highway after he had been forcefully removed from a hospital and placed on the highway by the police.

The injustice of the decision in *Winzar* is clear. The defendant did not voluntarily commit the offence and arguably should not therefore have had to bear legal responsibility for it. There are few absolute liability offences, so convictions such as this are rare. However, there are numerous strict liability offences. Strict liability offences are usually justified on the basis that they are for the public good, and they typically deal with issues such as public health and safety, protection of the environment and road traffic. There is the further advantage that court time is saved and costs are reduced when there is no need to prove *mens rea*. Those in favour of strict liability offences argue also that a higher standard of care is encouraged. However, there is no concrete evidence of this.

The legal profession, the judges and the legislature regard the principle of no liability without proof of fault as being especially important in criminal law. A guilty verdict will result in the imposition of a sentence on the defendant and in addition, arguably more importantly, a criminal record. The court has a wide range of sentences at its disposal, some of which directly limit the liberty of the convict, including electronic tagging, probation and incarceration. However, the liberty of the convicted individual is also affected by his/her criminal record, which may, for example, prevent access to certain jobs. The imposition of state sanctions and the restriction of liberty are generally regarded as justified only when the individual has been responsible for his/her actions.

The civil law is also based on the notion of individual responsibility. Individuals choose to behave the way they do and should therefore accept responsibility for the outcomes of their actions. However, while liability in civil law is generally based on proof of fault, there has been a shift towards no-fault liability in recent years.

Legislation of the twentieth century now provides a partial no-fault-based system. This is because the requirement to prove fault results in most accident victims not receiving any compensation. The Welfare State legislation created the Department of Social Security. Victims of accidents at work are now able to claim compensation from the state, without the need to prove negligence. Social security benefits are also available to those who suffer illness or disability. While such legislation provides compensation for more accident victims, it clearly penalises all members of society who have to pay for the actions of a blameworthy few. Since the enactment of the Consumer Protection Act 1987, producers have been strictly liable for damage caused by their defective products. However, although the producer directly provides the compensation to the claimant, the burden is indirectly borne by society. Producers inevitably recoup the money by raising the prices of their goods.

There are, however, many accident victims who are required to prove fault, including road accident victims and victims of medical negligence. It is argued that the cost of insurance would have to rise to unaffordable levels were no-fault-based liability to be imposed.

In conclusion, it would appear that fault should be a requirement of liability more so in criminal law than in civil law. The unfairness of leaving an injured victim without compensation increasingly outweighs the unfairness of blameless individuals being required to provide compensation out of state funds. In criminal law, however, the desire to protect the blameless individual from the outcomes of a criminal conviction makes imposition of liability without fault less acceptable.

This is a comprehensive, well-structured answer. Both aspects of the question, 'is' and 'should', are considered extensively and accurately. Excellent use is made of illustrative material throughout. This answer would be awarded 29 or 30 marks.

Balancing conflicting interests

To what extent can it be argued that the law can effectively achieve
a balance between conflicting interests?   (30 marks)

■ ■ ■

A-grade answer

In every area of law there are potentially conflicting interests. An important reason for
having laws is to set out rules, which should apply and ensure that all relevant interests
are considered and possible conflicts averted. For example, the rules on the making of
contracts or the rules on intestacy are designed to ensure that people know what they
have to do to ensure that their interests are protected.

The law also has to provide machinery — courts and tribunals — which ensure that if
conflicts of interest do occur there is a means of settling them in a way which tries to
balance the opposing views as fairly as possible.

In the nineteenth century, von Jhering suggested that society needed law to regulate the
conflicts that would inevitably arise between the many different interests and argued
that law acted as a mediator between these various competing interests. The American
academic Roscoe Pound suggested that there are two types of interests — individual
interests, such as owning property, and social interests, i.e. those that affect everyone
collectively. He also suggested that you can only balance individual interests against
other individual interests and social interests against other social interests.

By interests we mean rights or desires which a person or group might have. In some situations, e.g. a simple contract, there may just be two parties, both of whom have rights
because they are both bringing something of value to the agreement. In other situations
there may be a variety of interests of different kinds, e.g. when a paedophile is being
sentenced.

In some situations the law may have to favour one side in order to redress what is an
unequal balance, e.g. the statutory rules relating to implied terms under the Sale and
Supply of Goods Act 1994, and exclusion clauses under the Unfair Contract Terms Act
1977.

In practice, the courts do not follow Roscoe Pound's idea that you can only balance
interests of the same kind, and one way of considering how effectively the law is able to
balance interests is to compare public and private interests. On the whole, it could be
argued that where public and private interests are in conflict it is the public interest that
will prevail.

For example, in private nuisance the law is concerned to achieve a balance between an
occupier's quiet enjoyment of his or her land and a neighbour's legitimate use of his or

her land. In *Miller* v *Jackson*, the conflict involved an application for an injunction against a cricket club by residents whose properties adjoined the cricket ground. Lord Denning approached the problem in terms of 'a conflict between the interests of the public at large and the interests of a private individual'. Denning concluded that the public interest outweighed the individual one and refused to grant the injunction, although he did attempt to balance this by awarding damages to compensate for the inconvenience of having cricket balls regularly hit into your garden. This issue could have been approached in terms of one individual's private interest in enjoying his garden against the private interest of a group of people in playing cricket, but often the public interest is much more obvious, and involves an activity that benefits the community at large at the expense of a few individuals. In these cases there will often be statutory support for the activity. Railways, airports and motorways will all interfere with the enjoyment of land, but private interests will not be allowed to obstruct the public interest.

A recent example is the case of *Marcic* v *Thames Water* in which the claimant's house was regularly flooded with sewage. The House of Lords confirmed that the Water Industry Act 1991 excluded a remedy in nuisance. The balance here was clearly in favour of the public interest (the Water Companies), which would not be served if householders could demand expensive modifications to water treatment plants. On the other hand, the courts may be willing to award compensation where private interests have been damaged by public interests. In one unreported case in 2003, a householder was awarded almost £1 million compensation for disturbance caused by military aircraft from a nearby airbase.

Another obvious area of conflict between public and private interests is the protection of human rights, and the passing of the Human Rights Act 1998 would seem to emphasise the private over the public interest. However, often the relevant articles of the European Convention on Human Rights have derogation clauses specifically to allow the public interest to take precedence. For example, under Article 8 everyone has the right to respect for his private and family life, his home and his correspondence. Yet Article 8 also expressly provides that this can be overridden in the interests of things like national security, public safety, the economic well-being of the country or the protection of health or morals. In *Marcic* v *Thames Water*, mentioned earlier, an attempt to use Article 8 was rejected by the House of Lords. However, not all the rights in the European Convention are derogable. For example under Article 3, the right not to be subjected to torture or to inhuman or degrading treatment or punishment is absolute.

Furthermore, the courts do sometimes allow the private interest to prevail over the public interest. For example, in *A and others* v *Secretary of State for the Home Department* (2004), the House of Lords decided that the use of s.21 of the Anti-Terrorism, Crime and Security Act 2001 to detain foreign nationals without charging them was unlawful. Despite the public interest arguments put forward by the home secretary, the Law Lords stressed the importance of preserving private interests and protecting individual freedoms. A recent example is the decision of the High Court in *Mosley* v *News Group Newspapers Ltd* (2008). The claimant brought his action under Article 8 of the European Convention of Human Rights in respect of an article in the *News of the World* alleging that he had taken part in a sadomasochistic sex session with five prostitutes. His claim was upheld and he was awarded £60,000 damages, despite arguments in favour of the public interest in retaining freedom of expression and holding public figures accountable for their behaviour.

Another area in which we can see interests being balanced is consumer protection law. Here the role of the law historically was to establish rules to enable people to enforce contracts that they had freely entered into. Freedom of contract meant that the courts were reluctant to interfere with what the parties had agreed. But the resources and bargaining position of the parties in consumer transactions were clearly not equal and therefore the law, largely through statutory regulations, has intervened to protect the weaker party — the consumer. It is only in recent years that the consumer has been identified as someone with different interests to other contractual parties, most notably in legislation like the Unfair Contract Terms Act 1977, which does much to redress the imbalance created by the use of exclusion clauses, and the Consumer Protection Act 1987, which establishes what is in effect strict liability in respect of defective goods which injure people.

The need for balance can also be seen in criminal law. We can see the public interest in the need to ensure public order and protect the lives and property of citizens. Against this can be placed the private interests of individual defendants to have a fair trial and the private needs of victims who will want what they perceive to be 'justice' in the case. When we look at the whole range of provisions, we can see that the law is trying to achieve balance — certain activities are declared either through statutes or case law to be unlawful, and appropriate punishments are imposed to protect the public. At the same time, rules of evidence and the burden of proof protect the defendant, while victims are able to claim compensation from the Criminal Injuries Compensation Board, even if no one is convicted.

But the frequent changes to the rules by successive governments and almost constant discussion of law and order in the press and by politicians suggest that the balance in this area is far from effective. The previous (Conservative) government introduced the unit fine system (matching the size of the fine with offenders' incomes) in the Criminal Justice Act which was widely criticised because, although it tried to achieve balance by making fines more equal in their effect, it was seen as unfair. Equally, the Crime Sentencing Act, which introduced mandatory sentences in an attempt to protect the public, was criticised by judges as preventing them from being fair to individual offenders. The present government has made a number of changes to the criminal justice system in an attempt to achieve a more effective balance. For example, it has modified the right to silence and allowed the seizure of drug dealers' assets. It has also tried to restrict the right to jury trial. Specific measures to deal with the threat of terrorism have been even more draconian and, as seen in *A and others* v *Secretary of State for the Home Department* (2004), the courts sometimes seek to redress the balance. Nevertheless, the government continues to attempt to introduce new measures in the interest of public protection. Control orders, which impose severe restrictions on individuals' travel and communication with other people, in effect imposing house arrest, were introduced following the decision in *A and others*. However, the role of balancing conflicting interests played by the legislative process itself was evident when an attempt by the government to introduce legislation extending the maximum period a terror suspect can be detained without charge from 28 to 42 days was defeated. The House of Commons passed the 42 day proposal by a majority of just nine votes, but the House of Lords rejected the proposal by a majority of 191 votes. The government then announced that it would not try to force the measure through.

The problem is, of course, that the issues raised by these measures are hugely important. On the one hand, there is a danger that governments will use the excuse of crime or terrorism to increase the power of the state, while on the other hand, the private interests of the overwhelming majority of citizens as well as the public interest demand much tougher measures.

In conclusion, it is evident that achieving balance is not easy. In some areas, e.g. consumer rights, it could be argued that the law has been effective in achieving balance, but in many areas, particularly those where public interests are in conflict with private interests, the law has been much less successful in achieving an effective balance.

This is an excellent answer, which would be awarded 29 or 30 marks. It is well structured and proceeds in a logical, systematic way. The candidate begins by considering generally to what extent the law is there to balance interests, and never loses sight of the fact that this is what the question is about. A wide range of examples are used, from many areas of law, but they are always linked to the theme of balancing interests.

Reference is made to theories and they are also related to the examples. The relationship between public and private interests is particularly well explored.

The answer also addresses the issue of effectiveness and the essay is rounded off with a clear and thoughtful conclusion.